Wonder and Art: Cambridge Conversations With Tim Yip

Tim Yip and Alan Macfarlane

Cam River Publishing

First English Edition Published in Great Britain

By CAM RIVERS PUBLISHING LTD 2023
33 Trumpington Street
Cambridge CB2 1QY

WONDER AND ART:
CAMBRIDGE CONVERSATIONS WITH TIM YIP

Author: Tim Yip and Alan Macfarlane

Honorary Editor: Professor Alan Macfarlane FBA
Editor-in-Chief: WANG Zilan
Editors: Irene Galstian, QIN Yuchen
Student Editors: Sifan Guo, Yolanda Yujia Yan, Casey Niu,
Sirui Guo, Qianhao Han, Luofan Gan
Project Coordinators: LI Yue, Levente Koroes

Cover Photo by GUO Yushan
Cover Design: GE Dalong (MUYE)
Design and Typeset: QIN Yubin (MUYE)

The publishing of this book is supported by
the Vanishing Worlds Foundation, U.K.

A CIP Catalogue of this book is available from the British Library

ISBN: 978-1-916858-03-9
Contact: press@cambridgerivers.com
www.cambridgerivers.com

CONTENTS

Introduction to Cambridge Conversations with Tim Yip

In this introduction, I want to give some impression of the making of this conversation series with Tim Yip. A good way to start is from our diary entry on the 20th of January 2023 after my first meeting with Tim.

> A cool, crisp but sunny day. We spent most of it in Cambridge, going in by 11 o'clock to await the arrival of an amazing polymath artist, TIM YIP – see Wikipedia and his website. He arrived with a life-sized doll called Lili, who he takes everywhere, again see films on her on YouTube, etc. And then I interviewed him for 45 minutes, like digging down into ancient China. He was reliving the dynasties before Laozi and talked like a shaman, about parallel worlds, spirits, multiple visions and so much more. Sitting with me, giving a copy of *Letters to Lily* to Lili and talking to her. Felt a strange affinity with his ideas. A brother spirit. Very strange. He is famous, for his designs for costumes and sets for Ang Lee's *Crouching Tiger, Hidden Dragon*, etc. Look forward to another visit. Zilan seemed delighted, as did Sarah.

That account catches a number of the elements of what turned into six conversations, spread over a number of months, in which Tim and I talked to each other. After the first session, which was an interview, we decided that it would be more interesting to turn it into a dialogue, whereby I would ask Tim a couple of questions and he would ask me a couple. That worked extremely well. During the first dialogue session, we were beginning to get to know each other, and so it was a little more constrained. But as trust, knowledge and understanding grew, it turned into something really deep and meaningful.

There were a number of problems in this communication. Some of them were on my side. I am not an expert either in art, art history, design, film, or any of the subjects Tim mainly talked about. Nor am I an expert on Chinese aesthetics and ancient

Chinese philosophy. So, I was well out of my depth on many occasions. Yet the fascination of the subject made me struggle on.

On Tim's side, obviously, there were also great difficulties. One was that he was trying to talk about things at a level of the deep subconscious, which if you try to bring up into explicit language, you lose and distort. That's obviously a problem that all artists face when describing their work. How can you describe painting or music in language? So, Tim faced that problem, which was exacerbated by the fact that he wasn't just an ordinary artist, but someone who was trying to go deep into a layer and level which many artists don't even dream about. Struggling to bring that up and then to translate it into English, which he has learned from a child but is not his first language, was another difficulty. And yet he succeeded extremely well.

Those combined difficulties meant that occasionally we talked past each other. On other occasions, Tim would say very interesting things, but I couldn't at the time entirely understand them. As a result, I had to guess, sometimes wrongly, and often I missed the clues which someone else might have followed and gone on to a very interesting line of questioning. Tim also didn't know much about my world, yet I think I sparked his curiosity, and he seemed genuinely interested in a lot of what I was saying.

The result, which was in the form of six filmed interviews, was then transcribed using AI software. Irene Galstian did a magnificent job editing and simplifying the texts. This book is a tribute to her skill. It is also an indication of the fact that, despite the huge differences between the philosophies and aesthetics of East and West, there was enough in common between Tim and me to make for a meaningful conversation.

Certainly, I learned a huge amount about Chinese art and thought. It was a rare privilege to go inside the mind of someone who, as I described at the beginning, is a polymath, a photographer, a designer, a museum curator, a filmmaker, and much more. I found Tim to be versatile, interesting, unassuming, gentle, and friendly. So, it was a strange, difficult but hugely rewarding experience. The last thing to say is that, although I was not qualified in many ways for this endeavour, the fact that I shared an interest with Tim in exploring the borderlands between rationality and enchantment, which has been shattered to a large extent by modernity, gave us a common goal. We are both interested in exploring how and why our world is filled with wonderful and wondrous things. That is why we've sub-titled the book *Wonder and Art*. Tim's life, and mine, are filled with wonder at the strangeness and beauty of life.

Tim approaches this strangeness through many different forms of art, and I approach it through academic disciplines, particularly anthropology and history, in order to try to understand and communicate what I find. So, our methods are different, but in the end our goal is not dissimilar, namely to re-enter enchantment and see how it fits in our modern, fragmented, world.

I hope you will enjoy what we have jointly produced, also with the enormous help of Wang Zilan, who arranged the conversations. We would also like to thank Levente Koroes, who helped with the technical side, and Tim's PA Yushan Guo, who filmed and helped us to take Lili for lunches in King's College. Sarah Harrison checked the texts with her customary skill. To all of them, and particularly Tim, who added to his kindness permission to use some of his extraordinary artwork, a huge thank you.

Alan Macfarlane
August 2023

Spiritual DNA Drawing ©Tim Yip Studio

One. 20 January 2023.

Surreal worlds – Thinking and sensing energy – The world as a mirror – Being the space – Combining colours – Spiritual DNA.

AM= Alan Macfarlane
TY= Tim Yip

AM: It's a great pleasure – and surprise, I should say – to be meeting you. I am a great admirer of Chinese films, and particularly some of the ones like *Crouching Tiger* that you've been involved with. It's an honour to talk to you. When I went to your website, I saw that you are a modern polymath: a director, a designer, a photographer, a writer, a filmmaker – everything. You are my ideal of the Renaissance man. What I would like to do is to briefly go through your life to try and understand how it is that you are so distinguished and have done so many things, and to end up with your concept of New Orientalism which interests me. Tell me something about your parents.

TY: My father had always been the leader of the family. He was working in the gambling business.

AM: Gambling?

TY: Yes. My mother is from quite a wealthy family, and because she loved my father, she moved from a wealthy family to a fairly poor family. She was always away from the big family. While I was growing up, we were quite poor, and my father didn't start earning more money until he had a chance to work in Ho Hung-sun's company in Macau. Ho Hung-sun was the master of gambling in Macau. He was very famous there. After that we became better off.

AM: How old were you when you met this Macau gambling boss?

TY: I've never met him. My father worked with him.

AM: When did your father meet him? How old were you?

TY: Oh, quite young, maybe 15-16.

AM: Do you remember anything special about your childhood? Were you interested in pictures or painting or anything specific?

TY: Yes. I was always drawing. On any kind of paper. Even the exam paper. I would draw on every page of a book. But I always drew something strange. Not realistic things, always the surreal world, something connected with some kind of surrealism.

AM: That's very interesting. This is very similar to my grand-daughter, Lily. When she was two or so, she was always drawing. She's now a surrealist designer and an artist. One day I'd like to introduce her to you. She's an artist in Norwich.

At school, were there any subjects which you particularly enjoyed or hated?

TY: I liked sports, but I didn't do sports well. I don't know why. I have quite an active body, but I didn't want to exercise. I was very good at drawing, and I was famous in my school because of that. When I drew, people would come from other classes to have a look.

AM: Did you keep all those drawings?

TY: Some of them.

AM: I've got many of Lily's drawings.

TY: Wow… No, my father has several times thrown my drawings away because he was against me drawing. He wanted me to be normal. He felt I wasn't normal.

AM: So, he tried to stop you drawing?

TY: Yes.

AM: Were you living with your father or your mother?

TY: There were several periods. During my childhood and school years I lived with my father, and I had to hide all the drawings. If he saw them, he would just throw them away and stop everything. I liked comic books, so I would buy a comic book, hide it under my clothes and bring it into the house. Then I would hide in the toilet and draw the whole thing. I was always hiding someplace to draw, to escape from him. If he saw it, everything would be thrown away.

AM: Did you like Japanese manga?

TY: Oh yes, yes. It had a lot of influence on me.

AM: I thought so. Same with Lily. She loved manga.

TY: There is an intense feeling of freedom in manga.

AM: We all love Japanese cartoonists. Like Studio Ghibli, the people who made *Spirited Away* and all those films.

This is an almost impossible question… I'm puzzled why you, from being very young, were not interested in representing the world as you saw it, but you wanted to go into this surreal, alternative world.

TY: I think I've always had difficulty concentrating. When I was at school, I would just fly away while everyone else was paying attention to the lesson. I can't concentrate for too long, so I have to change focus all the time.

I always daydream. Even while at school, I imagined and drew every classmate and the teacher with very strange faces. I even got an award for that. From a very early age, people knew me for my quirky drawings.

AM: This surreal fantasy world, was it a constant sort of alternative world, like some of the great epics for children, like *Harry Potter*, or *Lord of the Rings*? Or was all your dreaming different all the time?

TY: They are more and more diverse now because I let myself fly in a way, even though I'm not doing such drawings anymore. I'm getting into the subjects of mythology and early culture. I like listening to music – ancient music. And I find that the world is not just the physical world. The physical world predominates when we concentrate on it. But there are many other layers. I see the physical world, but what interests me is how it becomes the way it is. There is energy that cannot be described using the knowledge we have. We have to feel it. I always communicate with that kind of energy, so that I can flow around with the physical world, but I'm looking for something more solid behind the physical.

AM: Are you a Daoist?

TY: Maybe. I am closer to being a Daoist. I have an elder brother who influenced me a lot. He became a Zen monk. He has shaved hair and every day he wears the robes.

AM: When you go into these fantasy worlds… Just to take this room: you are sitting in a room in Cambridge, which has many ghosts. These particular rooms are filled with famous people, for example Rupert Brooke, one of our greatest 20th-century poets; he wrote about Grantchester and so on. He was in these rooms here. Famous economists, famous scientists were all sitting where you are sitting now. Do you feel any presences of ...?

TY: I feel it very strongly. I can feel the ancient time. There is strong energy here. I don't believe it's gone because we have become modern. These old buildings have been here for many different time periods. I can feel the river, I can feel the building, I can feel the grass. Even the plants are different and have so much to tell me. I feel this energy very intensely.

There is intellectual knowledge, and there is sensing, feeling. Knowledge we can read and teach, and we can be taught knowledge. But to sense, you have to practise on your own to get to that level to feel it. Now I'm more concentrated on trying to wean myself off with regards to knowledge: I have to feel it. For instance, when I'm creating a sculpture, I *know* how it goes. And when I'm creating a sketch, I *know* how it goes. But now I'm making a movie myself, and I don't have a script. Now I want to *find* the shape of the sculpture, to *find* the shape that I have made deep beside that, like an empty space.

The Chinese call it *liu bai* (留白)[1]. Liu bai means the blank part of the drawing. When I draw one line, I change the whole surrounding area. So, I have to draw in another line to balance it. And then I would have to draw the third, the fourth. I *have* to, it's creating a balance – I don't have to *think* of anything. But at the end, when I find the balance, I just stop. I feel very clearly: this is the end of the drawing. I have drawn the 'spiritual DNA' drawings in this way, and I can draw a thousand more: each time I sense exactly where to start, where to stop. It's strange.

AM: So, when you are working very hard, do you go into an altered state of consciousness? When I'm writing, I forget time, I forget space. I sometimes explain that it's similar to what I've seen in the Himalayas, working with shamans. You go into a trance, and you feel something outside you working through you. You are speaking of this force. Do you feel it?

TY: Of course, every day. Every moment.

AM: Every moment?

TY: Every second. Because when you are talking, I am reflecting, reacting inwardly all the time on the energy level. When I am creating something, I'm reacting. I'm not doing what I *think* and what I *plan* to do. I don't believe in just holding on to things. When you are building something and want a result, you start planning actions to attain that result. But every result will limit

---

1 Lit. 'leaving blankness'.

the whole because things cannot be deliberately shaped. The real world cannot be shaped. If you want to fix something according to your plan and desired result, you can certainly do that, but in the act of fixing you will lose other things. So, how to create a way of keeping everything there, but in such a way that we can still follow it? To keep the full content, but without fixing it. I am seeing this again and again and again in truly great art. Every time you see it, you see different things. I think because things are not definite, you can, in your perception, see them anew again and again. People these days are talking about looking at things and deciding whether they understand them or not. It's about communication. But I think it's wrong because when we are talking so much about that, we are losing an important point: who is looking at these things? why don't they understand? Communication then reduces to low-level communication, like mass communication. It's not a high-level communication where you need very good eyes to look at something. Maybe the value in the work of art we are looking at is very different from what people will put into it nowadays. I think works of art have many secrets that we have yet to uncover. We've got to explore how to look at things.

I try to create an atmosphere conducive to sensing ancient art, for example in an exhibition I did in Minneapolis. I made the sounds, the lighting. I made abstracts. Art installations are experiences for myself. I wanted to invite people to see and try to feel first hand things that happened three thousand years ago.

AM: Three thousand years ago. So, before Confucius. In China or all over the world?

TY: In China. In Minneapolis they have a very good collection of Chinese bronze, one of the best in America. Shang dynasty. Exhibition pieces tend to be marked and described definitively and clearly, so that you don't misunderstand what the piece is. When you see a piece of art, you read the description, but you still don't know what that piece of art is. You don't feel it because you already think you know what it is because you read a description written by someone else.

Take a chair, for example. When we are talking about a chair, I see the trees. Maybe these are trees from Canada or maybe from other places. And I start to see – oh, some trees live in hot places and some in cold places, and so they have different colours. That will be what I see. But when you are educated, it seems like the chair is just the chair. You don't have to care or pay attention to where it came from. When you are living in a place full of names, you don't feel any energy. You just have intellectual knowledge.

I think it is very important to combine energy and knowledge together. It's like art and science. They always had difficulty combining and looking at the world together. But I believe these two are one thing, even though they seem different. There is matter, and there is spirit. What is substance? How does spirit turn into substance? I am always thinking about this kind of thing in my work and through my theories. You talk to me, and I feel Dao. Yes, something like that. It's very similar. Even Buddhism is different in China. In China, Buddhism is more like Daoism.

AM: Yes, absolutely. As you know, when Buddhism came into China it was very much altered. The form of Mahayana Buddhism in China is almost nothing to do with Buddhism in India or elsewhere. Or even Tibet or where I worked in Nepal. So many fascinating things you've said, and I'd like to talk to you longer. But I don't want to miss the opportunity to ask you what you mean by New Orientalism. One part of your work which interests me is trying to bring together Western aesthetics and art traditions and Chinese and Eastern ones. This is what I'm trying to do intellectually with my work in philosophy, politics and so on. And you're trying to do it with art. Is that what you mean by New Orientalism?

TY: I think New Orientalism means that I learn a lot of things from ancient China. From Zhuangzi, Laozi. I'm more that part. Zhuangzi talked about something that interests me very much. He talked about dreams and how he saw dreams and reality in a kind of mysterious relationship. Sometimes it's exchange: he would be looking at a butterfly, and he would say, 'I'm from the butterfly. The butterfly is looking at me.' It's like he's already talking about multi-universes.

If a multi-universe is the size of the Internet, it might still be possible to find a way to explain it or to find a way to the origin. But when you talk about dreams, it's very difficult. Right now, we are six people sitting in this room, but we are not sitting in one room. We are sitting in six rooms. Everyone is sitting in a different room, but it seems like we are together. When I see this room, I will see different things from you. You mentioned earlier that many great people sat in this room, and so, when I'm sitting there, you see not just me, but all these other people as well. What you know and think about these people affects the questions you ask me right now. It affects also how you interpret what I say in response to your questions because you are seeing me as many overlapping people.

Or take Lili.[2] She is not conscious, not a real person. But she looks like one. Most of the time you see her and at once have the feeling, oh, she is fake. But sometimes you go, *what is that???* It's suddenly seeing a real thing in a deep way. It gives us a chance to escape from the limitations of deliberately fixed, 'designed' consciousness.

One may talk about God, and I'm not dogmatic about such things, but I believe there is something true. Our design must have some reason. Why are we sitting here? Why are we facing all these problems? Why can't we be in harmony with nature? Why has this happened? I always thought we, human beings, came from outside.

AM: When you say outside, what do you mean?

---

2 As explained elsewhere, Lili is a life-size porcelain representation of a young girl. She was present throughout all the interviews. Her meaning is discussed extensively later in the interviews.

TY: Outside time. It's not the same system. But we are using nature because this has become a physical world. We borrow the physical world to let us into this time and space, and we bring our origin to the environment here, but this environment is very different from us. Human beings always fear the environment. And they don't know the environment. They started to create sciences, and it seemed like they could control everything. Then they started using this knowledge to shape the environment and use it for the things they need to build a perfect world for human beings. All our knowledge systems aim towards this perfect world. But as we look at the world we built, is it a perfect world? My theory is, the world is like a mirror.

AM: You use mirrors a lot in your work. Why is that?

TY: Mirrors are very interesting. When you believe in something, you will also see its opposite in the reflection. I do a lot of multidisciplinary work. Suddenly I would have the urge to put aside the movies and do contemporary art. Then I take in my work in contemporary art, and after that I might decide to do some writing. I always keep myself in a dangerous place to be able to use my true energy. Because when you are used to something you will corrupt yourself. You know what I mean? Your spirit will be corrupt because you start wanting things to be easy. That weakens you. Spirit is at its strongest when you are facing all the problems. When you are facing everything new. But then you find a way to make it harmonious. And after that you will feel, oh, the intensity has come down. Then it's time to go to another place. This keeps your spirit young. Without fear of being wrong, without fear of defeat. There will always be a way of finding the truth.

After doing some work, I work a lot on how to create myself again. I create myself in the multi-base, and then I make another movie with Lili, and I disappear again. Every artist, more or less, wants to create a self. Himself. You work this self into becoming the next work you are creating, because as you are working you have to concentrate on one specific thing other people can then read, see, experience.

I am influenced by Chinese philosophy. You have to be the space. It's bigger. When I am the space, I can have hundreds of angles to look at this room. But if I am myself, I have to direct my eyes to look here or there in this room. If I want to see from the top, I have to climb to the top and look down from there. And what is the top is a concept. In some ways, it is much easier to be inside a concept world. Concept worlds help us build systems to interact with nature. But at the same time, it is a kind of limitation. Maybe we are not that different from nature, but we separate ourselves from it because of the concepts we create. That's what I find.

There are so many things I want to talk about to the world. But the world now is becoming… I don't know how you feel about it, but I feel that it is more flattened. Because there are so many relations. So many related things. Of course, I express my thoughts freely here, which is very good, because Cambridge is a place where there were and are many original thinkers. Many original thinkers came out of Cambridge, and the powerful energy here is conducive to originality. I think as we talk here in Cambridge, maybe we can find active creative momentum originating from this place. Something powerful can come from such an origin. And it would be on a very high energetic level.

AM: That's why I like Cambridge. One of the reasons. All the time I walk around I'm seeing the people who have walked where you were walking. Charles Darwin or Isaac Newton or the discoverers of the double helix. When you were talking about art and science, I remembered the time when I first came to King's College and sat with a group of people who were all Nobel Prize-winning level. They were in arts, sciences and social sciences, and I was amazed that they could all speak the same language. Great mathematicians or physicists would look at a piece of work and say, 'It's beautiful.' They didn't say it was true. They said it was beautiful. They used aesthetic language. I have talked to and interviewed some of these great people, including those who believe in multiverses – they suddenly take you up to a level which is above science. It's somewhere difficult to describe, but it is at a different level.

One other thing I noticed is that a recurring theme in your work is the colour red. Rouge. Why is that?

TY: I think colour is like energy. It carries emotion. Sometimes I don't think in terms of this or that colour, but I feel emotion and match colours to it. When emotions are calm, I use blue or other cold colours. When there is a need to express intense emotions, the temperature of colours will rise too.

For a long time, I researched how colours are used in Chinese embroidery. There are many systems. Japanese is closer to the Tang dynasty. In general, individual colours and certain colour schemes have cultural origins. But with the rise of the commercial world in the 80s, of mass media and mass production, a lot of ideas were needed quickly to produce new things to excite and entice consumers. Creativity of cultures happens organically. It takes time and cannot be hurried. But the commercial pressure meant they couldn't wait, and many colour mixes appeared on the market to satisfy commercial demand that were not organically rooted in any culture.

But I still can find where the colour comes from when I see it. I separate colour into many layers. One layer is the colours that express imagination: even if I can't feel the signification directly, I can see the colour itself. And when I see the colour, I sense the intent behind its use. Another one is nature. Nature has original colours.

All the nations, because of where they live, have different kinds of colour schemes. European colour is harmonious. There is structure and also beauty, taste. In China there are rules of how to use colours. You can't just use any colour in any place. Certain colours must be put together, and they have specific significations. It's almost like a language.

All these sensations come together within me, and I put them into energy form to feel what is the energy being transmitted through these colours, how it worked within the original culture, and how it works with people now. So, each colour becomes easy to recognise, though how colours are put together is complicated. But I draw from the energy and so get to know the inner emotion. I think red signifies everything extreme because blood is red. In China, happiness is red. High intensity is expressed in red.

AM: You realise this is to do with your eye…

TY: Yes-yes-yes.

AM: The strongest signals for you are the red end of the spectrum, and for me it's the blue end of the spectrum. I've written a book about this, called *Glass*[3]. It's about mirrors, the influence of glass on eyes and so on.

I would like to ask you a question. In Hong Kong you are situated in the interface between the Chinese and the Western world. Much of my life as an anthropologist has been trying to explain to the West how people in other worlds live. I've worked in the Himalayas in Nepal, in Japan and in China. And I was born in India. Much of my work with Zilan[4] is about trying to create harmony between the East and the West. Because if we don't have that, we'll all be dead. So, my work is more in the political, social and economic fields.

But the problem one faces – I certainly do – is that almost every deep concept that I have is totally the opposite of your deep concepts. I live in a binary world, the oppositional, yes/no world from Greek philosophy down to the present. You live in a

---

3 Alan Macfarlane with Gerry Martin, *The Glass Bathyscaphe: How Glass Changed the World* (2002).

4 My colleague and former student Zilan Wang who made these interviews possible.

quantum world of both/and. For instance, I live in a world where the eye and the ear have become divided by the Renaissance. You live in a world where your writing and calligraphy are united. I live in an individualistic world that is based on me as a total person, separate and complete. You live in a relational – or what the French call structural – world, where everything is in the relation. It's not the individual things, it's the relational things. There are many more examples. I live with God all the time; you probably know, He is sitting here watching me now. You don't have Him there.

So, given that we're totally different, right at the level of basic thought systems and the way we look out on the world, how can the East and the West understand each other?

TY: Around 2018 I had a chance to make an exhibition. I worked with scientists in China, from the DNA expert group in the Academy of Sciences. Before that I had seen many different kinds of so-called art and science combined exhibitions. But I found they were still mostly in the technical phases as they're talking about how to do this. That is not what I was concerned with. I wanted to make an exhibition where, for the first time, art and science as I understood them would be truly combined.

We were in the lab with the scientists looking at how one cell gives birth to another cell from emptiness. But why does emptiness have these cells repeatedly coming up? I tried to ask one of the scientists, the experts, and then I said there must be something that we can't see between the cells. And he asked me, what is it?

That's how I created the term 'spiritual DNA'. Spiritual DNA means that we might see with our physical eyes that one cell is giving birth to another cell, but when we open our eyes to another level, we see something else underlying this process and making it possible. DNA is what builds up physical continuities and encodes the history of the organism. But underneath the physical there is the spiritual giving impetus to it. When we talk about the physical and search for origins, we might learn more if an earlier origin is discovered. But origin in the spiritual sense is not a question of earlier or later. It is, I think, something beyond physical. I believe the world is a form of energy. But when we are continually educated and told that the world is in a certain way, we eventually believe that the world is in this way.

Take this room, for example. It seems that we know it. Here we have a table. And we have a chair. But who chose this table? Maybe your young grandson would have chosen a brightly coloured table. And your wife, if she loves romance, would have chosen a delicate, ornate one. So, how the table came to be in this room is not just a matter of function, it's also where it came from, who bought it. In this way, when we see things, we would know how they came to be the way they are.

There are thousands of kinds of butterflies. Every dog is a different dog. Different dogs may be conceptually grouped into all being classed as dogs because of certain similarities in their DNA, but environment affects them, and a lot of differences appear between them. What is driving these differences? Is there something else like DNA, something we can turn into data and see the beginning and the end of this process? In thinking in this way, I try to understand another layer of the world, but this has already happened in China in ancient times.

They were always thinking about something beyond the physical. The physical is always not the whole of reality for them. They believed in ancestors: even when ancestors die, they are still here. They seemed to have a timeless view of the whole reality. They thought that they should behave well and do good things no matter how old they are. That they have to practise within themselves, so they could look at the world and know how to see the whole reality and not just the small things.

This is just like the things I am trying to understand: what is missing, or what are the things we still have to improve, or how to make ourselves even more free to get knowledge, free to know things, free to get creative power. I think for me the important thing is creative power. If you give creative power to a person, he will be positive and strong. He will solve the problem creatively. He will take care of everything.

The Chinese, as you know, say *xu shi bing zhi* (虚实并置). It means 'the intangible and the substance coexist'. How can people understand that? Quantum mechanics talks about this. We begin to understand that an event is not just happening there, in one place. We have to redefine what is happening there. We are looking at something, or we give another energy signal, and things come into existence. And they are not fixed. They are changing. I think at this point we need to find another way of seeing all this knowledge again.

And so, I painted many paintings with no thinking. Like meditation in a way. All of them different. Hundreds of different paintings, but you can see they are connected in some way. They are in some relationship, but we don't know what it is because I was not thinking anything when I was painting them. I discovered this relationship suddenly when I put them on the floor side by side. And as I looked again and again afterwards, I found more connections, more rhythm.

But I am just one person. Only me. How about other people when they are doing the same thing? How big is the world – we don't know. And then what is the relationship? There is so much more I want to tell you because I'm also taking photographs.

AM: Why don't you come back and tell me another time?

Gilbert and George in Love Infinity ©Tim Yip Studio

TWO. 26 APRIL 2023.

Talking about things vs making a space – Opening higher levels – Seeing Europe for the first time – Danger and creative energy – Book-learning and immersive learning – Origins and crises –*Love Infinity* and the real – Mirages of artificial intelligence.

TY: A lot to talk about.

AM: Yes. Are you living in London at the moment?

TY: I'm living in London most of the time, but I also live in Beijing for short periods of time. A lot of things are happening, and I have a lot of work there.

AM: So, you will go to China in June.

TY: Yes.

AM: For how long?

TY: Maybe one or two months.

AM: My wife and I are hoping to go in October.

TY: Where are you going this time?

AM: I like to mix big cities and remote countryside. I have some favourite cities like Shenzhen, Shanghai, Hangzhou. And we obviously have to go to Beijing, Chengdu. But also, we'll probably go to the very remote part of Sichuan, Kunming – for tea, the world tea centre. And there's one province in China we have not been to, in the middle of it. We have not been up to Xinjiang, and we've never been to Anhui.

TY: Oh, Anhui. I shot *Crouching Tiger* in the jungle there.

AM: Really?

TY: Yes. The bamboo forest is in Anhui. And the old buildings.

AM: How interesting. Everyone who's seen that film can see the bamboo forest.

TY: The style of buildings is different there. High-tower walls with narrow paths in between.

AM: We are told it's very important. There's also one of the famous Buddhist mountains… And we'll also probably go to a monastery in Jiangxi Province, near Jingdezhen.

TY: Yes-yes-yes. Fuzhou.

AM: Yes, Fuzhou. There's a monastery called Caoshan Monastery, and the nun who runs it is a friend of ours. I hope we'll visit her as well. Going to China is now like coming into Cambridge, because all the different parts have associations with our 17 visits there. And in each part we have friends. Usually young friends. They are wonderful. They are our closest friends now. They may be living in Shanghai or other places, but they always say to us, if you come anywhere in China, we will meet you. I have a filmmaker friend who is a very well-known film director now. She was head of Chongqing documentary films. She is in Chongqing now, I think. When we come to China, wherever we go, she will come and spend two or three days travelling with us, talking and catching up. It's really about friendship now in China more than anything else. But each time I learn a great deal.

TY: You have a deep relationship with Chinese culture.

AM: I feel at home. As you know, I have been told that I am a reincarnated lama, a Rinpoche, so I am really Chinese anyway, deep down. I feel immediately at home in China.

When I was a baby, I was brought up just on the border of China. In that area, and in Hong Kong and elsewhere, they have people called *ayahs*. *Ayah* is the nurse who looks after you when you are a baby. You have it all over East Asia. My mother had *ayahs* to look after me. And so, the first face I saw – and you know, you get fixed on the first face you see – the first face I saw was Chinese. So even now, whenever I see people with eyes like that, I feel warm towards them. And I find the Chinese so easy, straightforward, kind, honest – every good quality. I worked in Nepal among the people who have come down from northern China 2,000 years ago, and I came to love these people and always wanted to meet other people like that. So, I was delighted to find that there were not just a few thousand people like that, but all of China is like that.

When we go to China this time, we'll probably spend three weeks. I've also got several books which have been published recently in China, so we'll do book launches in a few cities, Shanghai, Wuhan, and others. I won't make any money from it, but it's just nice to meet and talk to people. We were there in November 2019, just before the pandemic.

Have you been all over Britain? Have you been to Scotland?

TY: Not many places. I'm in London mostly. I go to Wales sometimes and visit friends in nearby cities, but usually don't travel far.

AM: Sometime when you have time, come, and we'll show you a bit of the English countryside too. We are here just next to East Anglia, as it's called. It's just an hour away. This is Norfolk and Suffolk, on the coast. And it's a lovely area with a nice seacoast, the sea, and also many beautiful churches. And three or four wonderful old towns, because that area was very rich… with keeping sheep for wool.

TY: There were so many interesting moments when I was reading the way you talk about China in your books. It totally... It gives me a certain feeling. It's another angle, but I feel that what you talk about touches me closely. Our language is a little bit different.

AM: More than a little bit.

TY: When you think, when you talk, when you use words, the way you use them is so different, I feel.

AM: Well, I feel the same about Chinese.

TY: But we need that because I always feel how people in different cultures react to something. They're using their language to talk about this. I get a deeper understanding when I hear these different kinds of expression. They bring me to another angle of seeing the whole. And more and more, it's a good thing for me to understand how to express things back to the people who feel interest in Chinese culture.

AM: Well, if it helps you convey your message of what China really is to the West, because...

TY: It's a big job.

AM: It's a big job, and a lot of people are, even the Chinese government at the moment, very aware that, while they have advanced in many fields, the one that they are weak in is conveying the message and projecting China. This is because there's a double problem: a cultural problem, but also the hostility and misinterpretation. So, if you say something just slightly ambiguous to people who are going to look at it with a hostile gaze, they will misinterpret it. And indeed, China can't really win, because if it says something forcefully, then it's being aggressive, and if it says it humbly, then it's being feeble.

TY: The Chinese are different from the English in the way they explain and talk about things. The English, as they are explaining something, try to get more and more clear and instructor-like. But the Chinese try to make a space, to give the other person a space to reflect on something. They are not fixated on outcomes. So, it's difficult to explain what the thing is the Chinese are talking about, because the thing itself is not specified or discussed, just a space is prepared to approach the thing and reflect on it.

AM: Yes, you make a space. We just go directly.

TY: You talk about what is inside the space. We talk about the space itself.

AM: One thing surprised me. I worked a lot in Japan. I have a number of close Japanese friends, and when I offer to give them a copy of one of my books, I say, here's the Japanese version and here's the English – which would you prefer? They say, give me the English, it's much easier for me to understand. Japan is an extremely complex linguistic system – much more than China – with double and triple systems. And most of my friends say, reading Japanese is difficult for us, even as Japanese, whereas English is clear.

TY: I don't know why, but as intellectual knowledge is becoming more and more advanced, it becomes more difficult to understand things through such knowledge. Some things are just not accessible through knowledge of this kind. I don't know how to say it, but it's a different way of understanding... Maybe sometimes we can feel it, but we cannot feel it all the time, because we are in the physical world.

AM: Language, as you know, is a relatively poor form of communication. You can feel many things and see many things, which is one of the reasons why you use lots of different media.

TY: We can't say certain things. We can't make certain things clear. It's not easy.

AM: No, it isn't.

TY: Japan is interesting. I think we are losing some things in China, but in Japan they manage to keep them.

AM: Have you done many interviews like this before?

TY: Not like this. I do a lot of interviews, but not like this. Sometimes I like interviews, because even though I do not talk in an interview the way you and I are talking now, I still find some new questions for myself afterwards. But usually in the interviews

I talk about something not deeply enough. For the media, you know.

AM: This is a dialogue. That's what I like. I do lots of interviews, which are interesting, but in a dialogue there's some exchange.

TY: I believe in conversation because some things we don't know. If we don't have a conversation, we have no way of getting to know them.

AM: If one can have a cross-cultural conversation, that's the most rewarding kind of conversation because you have to make a leap across into another world, and, if you can do it, then you learn much more than if you just talk to someone in your own culture.

TY: Every conversation has a certain level. You have to open the space, and the level will be different. We could share even more. In early times they always had this kind of conversation to open higher levels of relating. It's like Kung Fu. There's always a relationship.

AM: It's the essence of the work I do as an anthropologist. More and more I realise that you learn most about another culture through conversations, even more than through the usual method which is participating and observing, being in the place and watching. It's the talking with people you trust and whom you get to know over time. In each culture I've worked in, I've got three or four such people. I can gradually get to know their world, and they can know my world. It's been particularly rewarding in China because I find it very easy to talk to my young Chinese friends. If we each ask one or two questions and then swap over back and forth – would that be okay?

TY: Yes.

AM: This, we hope, will be a significant conversation discussing the similarities and differences between two parts of the world,

China and the West, and, hopefully, because of your deep knowledge of Chinese history, philosophy and art, and my attempts over many years to understand the West and also China, there will be something productive. This is a very important time to do it because China, recently, in the last decade or two, has come back onto the world stage as one of the most important civilisations, as it was for many hundreds of years before. The West needs to learn something from China's great experience, as China has, over the last hundred years, been learning about the West. We are now like two brothers who are more or less on the same level and talking to each other. It's not an easy thing to do because of language, difference of background and so on, but, having met you before and having just been talking to you, I feel that it's worth attempting.

I'm going to start by asking you a couple of questions. Your artistic practice covers almost all areas of visual arts, and you transition between various roles such as director, designer, art director and curator. When you switch between these different roles and responsibilities, does each of them have an impact on the others? How difficult is it to do those switches between the different roles?

TY: For me, I think, it's the natural way of working. I work holistically, considering many aspects of the project and always asking the question 'what will it be like?' I have a dream of every project: when I see the trend that we are creating, I think of the most that I can do. So, sometimes when I do art direction, I also think of director's work and give a lot of information to the director. I give the structure of the story. I even refer to music. In my imagination I try to integrate every aspect of the film into the whole.

AM: So, for example, when you were doing your famous film with Ang Lee, *Crouching Tiger*, you weren't just concerned with the design of the sets. You did much more than that.

TY: Yes. I would start from the script and talk about the landscape and about the inner logic of various artistic elements. I would go deeply into what should happen in the time period the movie is situated in, the Qing dynasty, and if, for instance, the structure of the city in that period was different from the way it's portrayed in the script, I would point that out and ask them to change it. Ang Lee was very open to that.

AM: I was going to say, do they listen to you?

TY: Yes, they're open. We had a very good scholar there, and we would all get together to think about the script. When I was working on *Crouching Tiger*, I just had two months, so I was in a great hurry when I arrived. I started with the script because once the script was worked out, I could organically grow the whole language of the film. I always look for the origin. Even though as an art director I'm engaged in the last step, I must always think of the first step too. I always think of the whole film together.

AM: When you say you're the last person, you mean the designer is usually at the end?

TY: Yes.

AM: But you go back to the beginning and imagine everything from the beginning.

TY: I think about the whole film, not just the art direction aspect of it. So, when I am working as the director, I feel not so different because I think of the whole film anyway, whatever my involvement.

AM: So, all these roles that I mentioned are actually rolled together when you're doing things?

TY: Yes. The reason I went into directing is because I was not satisfied. Because otherwise the project would not be going totally in the direction I'd be envisaging. When you're working as the director, you can shape the project as a whole to a greater extent.

But at the same time, when you're working as the director, you lose some details because you don't have as much time to go into details as you did when you were in charge of just one aspect of the film. Also, I find that, at least in Asia, film professionals tend to be not really top level, though it's getting better now. You end up having to teach everyone, push everyone to a higher level, correct things. Your energy has to focus on all the details. But I'm used to it, I think.

AM: During your upbringing, Hong Kong was still a colony of a Western country and deeply influenced by Western culture. How did the 'Shanghainese' culture influence your work in Hong Kong culture? This is something which many people whom I've consulted about what I should ask you about asked. They said, one of the most interesting things is your Hong Kong upbringing and what influence that had on your work.

TY: At that time, as you know, there were in Hong Kong many Shanghainese who came from China. They seemed like people of a higher class. They always dressed well, talked well, went to beautiful places. They were not like ordinary Hong Kongese. They stood out. But at the same time, they were no longer at the elite level they might have been before moving to Hong Kong. It was different from when they were in Shanghai. They always got together and spent time with other Shanghainese. They were aware that they were different. Even the way they served tea and other things like that were different.

AM: All the details were different.

TY: Yes. It was obvious they must have come from another place; they certainly were not from Hong Kong. And so, we paid attention to them. Afterwards I found that we had a dream of the West. When I lived in Hong Kong, the European art scene was very vibrant. They had already established modern art and were actively moving forward from Impressionism. There were many interesting things in New York, in London, and in many other places. We in Hong Kong had a feeling of looking forward to it.

In earlier times the Shanghainese were to us a way of mixing the two cultures together. Through them we received all sorts of ideas from the West, and they made us dream of the West.

That's why, when I was young, I packed my bag and went to Europe, to visit and see many European countries for myself and meet the people as much as I could. And I understood what is inside me, which attracts me deeply to this kind of beauty.

AM: You went to an English-medium school, is that right?

TY: Yes. A Christian school.

AM: A missionary school. That must have influenced you.

TY: I quite like the story of the Bible.

AM: You do?

TY: Yes. It's deep. I have a good feeling about it. They talked about miracles, about the human soul and things like that. And about Jesus dying for the people. I think it is a very deep thing.

AM: But you're not a Christian. You've never been a Christian.

TY: I think at that time, for a short while, Christianity attracted me, but not in the religious way as such. That involvement was not very deep, I think, but I feel strongly about the Bible because it has so many stories before history. There is a wide range of information in the Bible, and it is different from other mythologies. And the Bible had so much influence.

AM: Well, that's one way in which the West was deeply influencing Hong Kong. In other words, language and religion, but also law, civil service, policing, governmental system, financial institutions. So, it's intersection at every level. You mentioned that Shanghai was also like that in the Western-influenced part. Do you think you looked at the West mainly through things in Hong Kong, the institutions I've been talking about, or through Shanghai and the way in which the West had come to Shanghai and influenced it?

TY: I think Shanghai came later because I worked in movies, and we always researched the time period the film was set in. I worked on several movies about that period and got deeply into the research of this part. But before, in Hong Kong, I always felt unsatisfied, I think because the information we were getting about the West was not coming first hand. It was changing in the process of transmission, and important things were missing because they just showed us a little bit. I felt deeply dissatisfied with that. I wanted to see Europe, so I could go and see for myself everything that influenced me. And then finally I saw Europe with my own eyes and visited all the places I wanted to visit. You go through the journey; you sleep in trains. Everything happened on a deep level in my mind during that visit.

AM: At what age did you first go to the West?

TY: Maybe early 20s. And I felt everything is mine.

AM: Everything is yours?

TY: Yes, it's mine. When I saw Van Gogh and other Western art, I felt on a deep level within me that this is my work. After I visited all the museums, I felt, wow, I have done a lot of things. And the art I saw affected what I was thinking and creating. I think it's about the energy. The mystery of innermost emotion. I can sense it. Like Da Vinci's *Mona Lisa* – I feel it very intensely.

AM: I hadn't thought of it, but because of growing up in Hong Kong, you felt in a way that Western art was not unfamiliar. It was yours and belonged to you. And I realise now that I feel the same about the East because when I was a child, I spent my first five years in India. Going back to work in Asia, I don't feel it's totally strange. I understand something about it, as if I was half there and half here.

TY: I always jump straight into the intensity of feeling. I skip explanations and other conceptual things and go right into the intense energy. Many kinds of intuitions can come together in this way because they are not weighed down by concepts and separations. When we conceptualise, things get knocked down into points. But when I just feel energy, I can put all the energy together directly. There are no limitations, no storage problem, so to speak. And all the time you feel almost the same. Everything is the same.

AM: Universal.

TY: Yes. There is a question that interests me very much because I'm from Hong Kong. I would love to hear how you feel about Hong Kong and China in the cultural sense. You meet young people from Hong Kong, and you also meet young people from mainland China. What's the difference between them from your point of view? I mean, the young generation, because they grew up in different places.

AM: Well, I've been to Hong Kong. In fact, on my first visit in 1996 we went to Hong Kong, and I've been back there four or five times since. It does feel a strange place to me because it's half familiar. It's half like going to an English town, the layout of the streets, the language, the names of shops. That's very familiar to me because it was the same in all of British Empire: when you go to parts of India, to the hill stations and so on, you have the same feeling. You feel, this is very familiar. And yet, it's a bit like the types of curry that I like, say Thai curry, which has a bit of China and a bit of India mixed together. It's sort of half-and-half. I found it a very exciting place for other reasons as well because some of the people I worked with in Nepal were recruited into the British Army. They were Gurkhas, and they were often posted to Hong Kong, so when I did go to Hong Kong, I didn't go to a place with no one I knew. I suddenly found these Chinese-derived people I'd known when they were children and growing up. They were still in the Hong Kong police and so on. So, I found it exciting, and we bought various things in some of the old art shops. I was impressed, and I loved it. I love the food and I love the harbour and going back and forth. I always look forward to going to Hong Kong. So, that's my answer on Hong Kong.

TY: So, you feel the Hong Kong young generation and the mainland young generation face differences in terms of inner development?

AM: Yes, from what I gather, I think they do, which is sort of sad. But then, when you think of the size of China and you think of the difference of someone in Liaoning or Beijing and someone down in Kunming or Sichuan, it's the same sort of large cultural differences as between Mandarin and Cantonese. It's no different from any other Chinese province, really, except it's had more British influence.

TY: I want to ask you about the beginning of your acquaintance with Chinese culture, for example the Kun opera. How did you encounter the Kun opera?

AM: My wife and I first saw the Kun opera in Suzhou. I knew nothing about it before but had been to see Peking opera in Beijing, which was harsh to our ears. With Kun opera, I've learned to really love it because it is very gentle, filled with colour, as well as sound. We saw *The Peony Pavilion*. Very romantic stories. It's not dissimilar to one or two of Shakespeare's plays – *The Tempest*, for example. The author died in the same year as Shakespeare. It's a love story filled with dreams. Kunqu, like all Chinese opera, is actually much older in its form, it has preserved fragments of pre-Confucian China woven into it. And therefore, when one watches it, one has a sense of going back thousands of years. And also, it dissolves, it's dreamlike. In fact, a lot of it is set around the theme of dreams. And it therefore appeals to my idea that Chinese culture doesn't make the strong separation between dreaming and ordinary life. You move easily between them. Nor between death and life – like the theme of coming back from the dead. It dissolves all separations which we have in our culture, and therefore, at every level, even if you cannot understand a word of it, you can really appreciate it. It was a particular delight having the Kunqu opera here in Cambridge and seeing ladies in these wonderful fairy dresses floating across the back lawn of King's.

What other fields do you want to challenge in the future? Cross-disciplinary projects, for example? What breakthroughs do you want to make beyond what you have already achieved?

TY: Now I am deeply involved in developing total art. This means combining everything. For example, I just finished a project directing a total art creation, and there I combined filming techniques with stage techniques and integrated them together. Sometimes I develop aesthetic language into something sort of abstract. It's not like the normal language of theatre or the normal language of movies. I always want to develop something new because I don't believe that the system that exists is enough. I always want to try something more: a new language, a new way of communicating.

AM: You've used photography, you've used film, you've used music, you've used design – all the different media – and directing. Now you're trying to put them all together. What will you do after that?

TY: I really love coming to Cambridge. Here I feel like I want to put everything down and start anew. That's what I want to do next.

AM: That is a very sensible approach because you get to the end, like walking along a path, you get to the end, and you can't force yourself further along that path. You need to go back to the beginning and walk another way.

TY: Yes. It seems like when you go somewhere you will eventually be walking in circles in that same place. I don't know why humans do that. You will walk around in the same place for a while, and then you have to do something different, to become lost. At that point you will find a new way. I've been doing this for a long time. Testing different things. I put myself in a dangerous position, and in that state of danger I have full energy to create a new way to re-balance. After that balance is settled, I find that I am in another place, and I find another thing to express. That is what I want to keep doing.

AM: In my case, when I've been writing a book and more or less finished it, I try and choose a subject which is a long way away from what I've already done and about which I know nothing. More and more I realise that you come to an understanding when you face something that is completely unknown to you, and in that period of explaining whatever the phenomenon is to yourself, in researching it and writing about it is when you learn new things. If you already know most of it or have done it before, it becomes stale. My favourite description of creative processes is by the Scottish philosopher and founder of modern economics Adam Smith, who said that creativity lies in wonder and surprise.

TY: Yes.

AM: There is the surprise that the two are linked, and the surprise of suddenly encountering a whole new landscape which before that you didn't know existed. You can't do that by sticking within a safe area.

TY: Yes. When there is risk and danger, your energy rises. When you're safe, the energy is closed.

AM: But it is dangerous. You're so famous now that it doesn't matter, but in my world of academia younger scholars are threatened if they go off into new areas. They're sacked from their job or don't get a promotion. But you are a free spirit.

TY: I face a lot of problems that other people don't have, because I am always unstable, uncertain. I live with uncertainty because I like that kind of energy and so that I can try even more things. It's like growing my IP (Intellectual Property), so if people like something of what I did in the past, they are more willing to believe that I can do something more in the future, and then I get an opportunity to try something new, and when I do something with a new thought, there is a better chance that people would support me.

I think this is the way that I want to develop because cultures in modern times are shrinking. They are getting smaller and smaller, more and more people don't understand, and they are more and more distant to what happened. People are losing the content. There is no longer any content. Traditional culture is from content, but now the content is disappearing. And everything is happening, happening… things are being repeated that happened before, but there is no content.

AM: When you say 'content', what do you mean?

TY: Content is when you're doing something, and you have an underlying principle. Content means the essence of what happened. In traditional art, they might talk about life, they talk about culture, talk about relations with family, they talk about the way of acting, they talk about technique, they talk about the total art. But now there is no essence: when someone has a red face, they just have a red face, that's all. And when they have a certain discussion, it's just a discussion; they don't understand what this discussion is about. Things are expressions from a certain period in time. I express that I'm crying by having very long sleeves because I use the movements of these ultra-long sleeves to convey my sadness and despair. But now this has become a technique, a formula – it is no longer an expression. They can't tell the modern story now. Everything is fixed into a form. There is no expression. This is what I mean by losing content.

AM: I see.

You not only have many well-known film and television works with Chinese themes, but also participated in European and American operas. These works are products of different themes and cultural backgrounds, but you seem to interpret them almost perfectly. How do you achieve a deep understanding of other cultures in a relatively short time and realistically reproduce the stories that took place in a specific time and environment?

TY: I'm deeply interested in human history. In internal feeling, psychological and philosophical. And also physical. When I was quite young, I researched a lot. It seemed like I wanted to know everything. Even now my house is like a bookstore. I'm crazy about books, about knowledge.

AM: The house in London or in China?

TY: China. Before it was in Hong Kong, then I moved to Taiwan and then to Beijing. So, now the Beijing house is full of books.

AM: How many books do you have?

TY: I have about 30,000. Even more.

AM: And I thought I had a lot. I've only got 22,000.

TY: That's a lot of books.

AM: Do you have any way of storing what you learn from the books? Like any kind of indexing system or notes or another way of connecting.

TY: I am interested in such things and want to learn, but I have already tried different systems a number of times, and each time I mess it up. I buy many books, but I'm not reading all of them because I have no time. A lifetime would be needed to finish reading them all. But I still buy books to read later if there is an occasion. Some books you cannot find anywhere else. You see unusual content, and so you buy the book, and having these special books makes you different from other people.

Afterwards, I have my way of putting them into relations. It's all about relation. I have different kinds of books: Chinese, Japanese, European, African, Indian, Mexican. I separate them geographically. And I also go from old times to modern times.

I always find that books have a dialogue. All the books have a point of view, and each book has a dialogue with the reader. When a culture becomes powerful, it might produce hundreds of books. A less powerful culture or maybe one that is located far away from mainstream will produce very few books. You can find almost nothing about it. Our knowledge is being shaped by the more powerful sources. The more powerful sources, like the English-speaking cultures, are very forceful because they have dictionaries or encyclopaedias where everything can be looked up. German culture also has this tendency of encylopaedia-like books.

We learn from such books. And we learn to understand in two ways. One way is for me to understand internally what Kunqu is. But I can also look it up in the dictionary, read the description there and learn what Kunqu is in that way. We are lucky because we have two ways of looking at anything. We can look up the dictionary to find out the scientific way of understanding what is the Indian, what is the Thai, and their differences. We can find them in the categories of the dictionary form of knowledge. And after that we could go to see the culture and understand the immersive part of it. It's very nice. I have been visiting many performance festivals with old music, old-style performances and costumes that I can learn from when I see them and feel the music. We can visit one place and see many different cultures together at that kind of festival.

AM: Have you been to our Museum of Archaeology and Anthropology yet?

TY: No, but I'd love to go.

AM: We'll go and have a look. That's an example of this sort of thing.

You mentioned different spaces in your house, Japanese and others. What languages can you read or speak?

TY: I can't read Japanese. But it's very good that we have digital translation now. It helps a lot. I can speak and read Cantonese, Mandarin and English.

AM: You mentioned that you tried many systems of indexing or absorbing your materials. Did you ever try any computer-based systems?

TY: I did. The system I have now is computer-based, but I have a lot of trouble with computers. I don't know why, but when I work with computers, they give me a shock. Or they are not working. I really like traditional things.

AM: You have too much energy, that's the thing. You're blowing the computers up.

TY: Traditionally you put things in boxes. And then you simply take things out of the boxes and read them. It's physical. But with the computer it seems like you have to control it in another world, and it gives you back the information. That's difficult.

You mentioned the Digital Museum. Can you talk about your plans for it?

AM: For some reason, since I was a late teenager, I've been interested in multimedia. I've been interested in the problem that you can't convey knowledge very well just with words, and therefore you need films, music, sound and so on. So, very early on in my life I experimented with lecturing using slides and films. Then in the 1980s there was always a problem bringing together the visual and the textual. With the computers which I was working on, it was more or less impossible because you couldn't store images in a computer, and you couldn't access them.

Then around 1983, the Japanese produced a new form of media, the first generation of video disc. On the video disc there are 37,000 tracks, each one of which can hold either a still image or sound. If you just put moving film on, at 25 frames per second, it would hold 37 minutes' worth. But this, which is the first academic video disc in the world, we made here in Cambridge, and it has 10,000 black and white photographs on it, and about 10 or 15 minutes of film, and also a lot of music and sound. You put it in a player and then you can see or hear them.

There was no way you could type in a number and go to the corresponding media item; it's direct access, the first direct access medium. But they hadn't thought much about how you could use this. So, I developed a project over a period of about five years, where I took a society, a tribal society with a fantastic art system, beautiful carving, clothes and so on. Beauty was at the centre, although they were a very warlike culture on the border of Burma and India, the Naga people. My professor had a lot of films and photographs, so I had access to some wonderful materials.

TY: What year was this?

AM: 1986. My idea was that you should use all the different media. There is a book which we've got here, with many illustrations, so you have the book.[5] You have a museum exhibition, which we did in the Museum of Archaeology, a whole gallery where we reconstructed a communal meeting place, a boys' dormitory, wood – we had carved wood. You had many of the wonderful objects in the museum there. And people could go inside. You had the computer screen, and you could choose clips of film to watch. They were doing it in a Japanese museum in Osaka at that time too with video discs of different cultures. But what the Japanese hadn't done was to connect a computer; we showed them when we visited in 1990.

Since then, I put lots of stuff on YouTube and made lots of films.

5 Julian Jacobs and others, *The Nagas: Hill People of Northeast India* (1990).

Since then, I put lots of stuff on YouTube and made lots of films. It's more and more obvious, particularly with COVID, that the world's treasures, whether it's tea, Buddhism or Kunqu opera, should be shared by the world. You should be able to sit in any culture and see them. Part of our aim was to return treasures to where they came from. Much of your Chinese culture is here in Britain, as you know, not in China – or in America, or in France. We should be returning it. So, one of our projects, one of our dreams, is really to make international databases, which would make it possible for Chinese to see Chinese cultural objects that are located outside of China.

TY: I just came back from Minneapolis to do an up-and-coming exhibition, and there they take very high-quality video of the art pieces. You can see the video playing on the screen, and it's extremely detailed. You can also see it on the Internet – it's open to everyone.

AM: There are all sorts of new possibilities.

TY: I have a question about the exploration of time by Western Christians. In early Christianity they still had circular time because it was promised that Jesus would return. It seems like the concept of time they had was built around the return of Jesus. I put Lili into my work as the grey area of time. We all have to deal with physical time. We mark time. But what about spiritual time? Do you have an opinion on the spirit of time?

AM: In most of history, 99% of history, time was very short and circular. In tribal societies you don't have any written history, so you can't go back in time. In one African society, for instance, people until recently said, well, that's where our society came from, under that tree. That tree was here at the beginning of time, like the Garden of Eden. And it's only a few generations since we came and lived under that tree, seven-eight generations. The sort of universal view of time – to a certain extent in China, but certainly in Western thought – was that time was circular; it was like the seasons. You have winter and then you have winter again – you always come back. And even in Middle Eastern thought, in the work of the philosopher Ibn Khaldoun, it was three or four generations, and then you came back to the beginning again. So, as the Bible said, there is nothing new under the sun, because everything has happened before. The Renaissance, in a way, was a break with that, because before that everything went back... So, that's the first model of time.

The second model of time was around the 15th-17th century, after the discovery of America. Suddenly whole new civilisations were discovered that weren't anticipated in the Bible, and discovering new things which the ancients didn't know about. And so, in the later 16th-17th century you get the idea of *progress*. There *are* new things under the sun. We can, with modern science, make and discover new things. There are the old things, and there's the future.

Then, in the 18th century, time began to become progressive. So, you have the metaphor behind the Enlightenment. In other words, it's dark there, light here, and we are moving from darkness to light. We have progress, and we have upward movement. We can do things they couldn't do. So, time becomes progressive.

And then there's a period of despair in the West, which is the result of the industrial revolution, the horrors of new cities and also the terrible Napoleonic wars. And the French Revolution above all, because here man's hopes are crushed in what actually happens if you follow Rousseau. You get a period of about 40-50 years where everything falters.

But from the 1830s-1840s things begin to improve.

TY: The second industrial revolution?

AM: Yes, it starts to kick in, and the West becomes dominant over the whole world with the British Empire and so on. And so, you get the great phase of evolutionary thought for about 50 years, with Darwin and Spencer: anything is possible, the West is years, with Darwin and Spencer: anything is possible, the West is up here in development and China is somewhere down there. It's another concept of evolutionary time

And then, around the end of the century, doubts start again. They reach their peak in the First World War because the most enlightened, rational nations on Earth just slog it out for four years, killing each other. Suddenly we are not superior: Japan is coming up here, India there. So, time flattens, goes static again. This is a period in social sciences which is called functionalism. You're not concerned with the origins of things or the evolution of things. You're concerned with the here and now. What does this do? What does this table do? Not where did it come from. Functionalism is the great period of anthropology and continues to a certain extent in structuralism, French structuralism, which is against time: there are layers of meaning and language but no development, really.

But there are two counter-strands. One is Marxism, which is evolutionary; it was developed in the evolutionary period. In certain parts of the world it's believed that we are on the Marxist path. And the other, American power after the Second World War means that you get, in American anthropology and elsewhere, the idea that we are 'taking off'. So, there's a muted form of evolutionism again.

After all that, everything dissolves into chaos and postmodernism.

These five or six different concepts of time fit with different social systems and different technologies, so at the moment it's very interesting to think about what artificial intelligence and modern communications are doing to our sense – well, the young people's sense – of time. I think it's fragmenting it hugely and making it very difficult. And also cutting them off from the past more and more. Anything that happened before mobile phones is really nothing that they're interested in. That's my answer on time.

You've lived in London for a long time and travelled the world with Lili. What are the differences in expression and demand for art among people in different countries and regions? What kind of inspiration do different art atmospheres bring you? These are two questions really, about the difference of aesthetics of art between the East and the West.

TY: I think Western society has seen a lot of contemporary art, and so people would be more accepting of that kind of expression. Also, people in the West already have a basic concept of things like performance art or installation art. In China people think more about real things and people. They would be looking at, say, an artistic depiction of a real person and responding to that expression, but they are not as open to the contemporary art language. It's different.

AM: Going further into the differences over history in the aesthetic and art systems of the East and the West… Say, from the Renaissance, how would you describe the main differences between Chinese art and Western art?

TY: I think that, as you said, the basic structure of society, the world view, the role of family, relationships and class are very important. The West has been educated for many years in an international way, but in China, or more generally in Eastern cultures, I think the traditional and the contemporary ways of thinking are farther apart. Eastern cultures have to learn or to find the meaning of the contemporary. The contemporary way has not developed organically within these traditional cultures. It is part of globalisation. It's interesting to observe the traditional reactions to this new international tradition. There is a gap, but now people are more and more accepting of the international because it is getting increasingly closer through the Internet and the many things that are shared worldwide now.

AM: My impression was that art systems of the world were very similar until the Renaissance. In other words, all art systems were basically symbolic. The objects in the paintings represented something else, God or Christ, or mountains representing

Buddhist philosophy or something like this. That was to be found in iconic and other art systems. Then there was this big break in the Renaissance in the West, and the West went towards realist representational art, almost like a camera photographing things. But not in China. They could have done that, but they decided they didn't want to. In Chinese art, when the Chinese look at a painting of the earlier periods, they don't just see a bit of wispy cloud and a mountain and a few willow trees. They see Tang poetry, and they see allusions. Everything is pointing to something else. Whereas we see a face, an old man, or whatever. Am I right in thinking that's the great difference?

TY: Western art changed considerably in the Renaissance period. Before the Renaissance the main subject of art was God. Everyone worshipped God, and art reflected that. Then there was a transition towards individualism, which led to some diversity. That led to the development of science and trying to understand the thought in the art of dream. After that people became more individualised, doing more surreal art and going deeper into the subconscious, which created even more diversity.

But in China they didn't develop that because, just as you said, the structure of society is relational, and individual differences are not encouraged. Even though there were many painters in ancient times in China, and they did have different styles, the content of the paintings is quite similar. There was a big enough space for everyone to be in, and the differences were in the artists' spiritual levels and their way of facing emptiness. It's about how deep you can go, not how different we are.

AM: Right. You mentioned the concept of 'spiritual DNA' and that Lili is an artistic incarnation you use to express time depth. Can you talk about your understanding and thinking about time and space, existence and illusion from the perspective of ancient Chinese philosophy? …It's a big question. Ten questions in one. You can choose any of them.

TY: I mentioned earlier the collaboration with DNA experts from the Chinese Academy of Sciences when I saw in the lab how one cell gives birth to another from emptiness. I knew about that theoretically, of course, but seeing it was shocking. I think there is an invisible force, which I called 'spiritual DNA', that makes it possible for a new cell to appear from nothingness, but scientists can't think in this way because they are dependent on experimental data, which they don't have yet. But an even more interesting thing for me was that the new cell, even though its form repeats the form of the cell that gave birth to it, is also different from it. These differences made me think about time. My understanding of time is that it has no continuity. Each instant is individual. But how do they become time as we usually experience it? Let's say I make a motion with my hand to brush a small speck of dust off my face. There is an instant of time when my hand is here. Then an instant of time when my hand is touching my face. Then another instant, and another. 'Between' instants there is emptiness, and an invisible energy is in this emptiness. My hand 'moves' from here to my face because I am thinking. Continuity of time is an effect of our own thinking. So, when I see the physical world, it's just facts.

AM: Just a face.

TY: Yes. It's like when I see you when you are happy, your face would be radiant. But when you are unhappy, your face would look sad and tired. It's not about the face on its own, but about something within you affecting it. This is what really exists. The fact is just a fact. It worries me when people insist on always thinking about the facts. They are missing very important things.

Say, for example, a talk is to be given in this room, for which I need 20 chairs, and so I look for and find these 20 chairs. When you use spiritual DNA to look at these chairs, you, as I said earlier, see that some of them are made from trees growing in Canada, others from trees in the Philippines. You experience the different textures and colours of the wood, which were formed by the different conditions in which these trees lived. It may be that a tree is transformed into a chair now, but the connection with the living force of the tree remains, and with it a spiritual component. Looking at the chair in this wider way would make you care about being responsible towards the trees, about how and where the chair was made, about how the chair makes people comfortable, and everything involving this chair would transform too and become spiritual because everything is related.

But nowadays the tendency is to define the world by commercial concerns and to put human needs at the centre of everything. The chair is reduced to a number. We don't care where or how the trees lived. We just need the lumber. Living trees are turned into faceless 'resources', and the chair becomes to us just a function. Our narrow and superficial attention cuts the chair off from the living energies of nature, and so we, human beings, cut ourselves off from these energies too. Now there is much discussion of environmental crises and things like that. The deep question underlying all this is how to get back the connection, the content, and to realise that content, and not the function, is the important thing.

AM: Indeed.

TY: I have a couple of questions. As we know, theatre and cinema belong to different generations, and theatre is earlier. But China is opposite to England, because in England people prefer theatre rather than cinema, whereas in China people will all go for cinema and have little knowledge of theatre. What do you think about this difference? Is it because of something in the English culture?

AM: Well, it's an interesting change, because if you read 19th-, 18th-, 17th-century Chinese history, theatre is the centre. They had travelling theatres. I'm editing a book on the 19th-century missionary Évariste Huc, who travelled over China. He said, in every town, every village you go to, they have a theatre. People paid little bits of money, and the attendance was huge. You had this double tradition, you had theatres everywhere. And sometimes music, like Kunqu, but sometimes just plays. And you also had people, the storytellers, who went round to villages and towns, stood in the middle of the square and recited stories. For example, Yeh Chun Chan, who was at King's, described his boyhood in his books about China in the time of the Civil War in the middle of the 20th century, and these traveling orators were still around at that time. There was obviously no cinema anyway. So, China, like much of East Asia, has a great theatre tradition, I think. More than here. We did have some theatre, and it goes back quite a long time, but it wasn't as important as it was in China when you had no other kind of entertainment. But there's been a big switch. You would know when this happened. Cinema was used for propaganda during the communist period, and there was a little bit of cinema before. But it's recently become the medium in China, whereas in England, even though more people go to the cinema than to theatres, we do have a very strong theatrical tradition. It started just a century or so before Shakespeare; derived, most people think, from religious theatre of various kinds. And then, in the Elizabethan period, it was very strong. The English, on the whole, are not among the greatest of artists. In music, there is Germany; in art, the Netherlands, Italy, and so on. But our greatest arts are theatre, novels and poetry; speech – because the English language seems very well adapted. We have many of the great dramatists and novelists and poets. And partly because our social structure, though changing all the time, remains very constant, you can still take people to 17th-18th-century plays, and, although the language is a bit strange and archaic, the sentiments are relatable. Anyone can go to a Shakespeare play and feel, yes, that's me, I can feel that jealousy or that pain or that love. And so, these early dramatists are alive. This is, I think, a little different from most countries, because they've changed so much that the theatre of earlier periods doesn't appeal to them. Looking at the French, for example, the period of Corneille and Racine seems very strange now, from another time. But we can just put on Shakespeare, and it lives for us – or Jonson, or Marlowe. So, partly because we haven't changed in that deep nature, our theatre is at the heart of our culture. Cinema we like, but it's not quite as important. I think if you put this question as saying, why is theatre *symbolically* more important for English culture, since in terms of numbers, cinema is more important.

TY: My understanding is that in China the audience is more passive. People may go in to be educated or to be entertained, but their position is that of reacting. People don't go in with their own expectations. They react to what they are shown.

But in the West, people are always asking questions or sharing their opinion. A more active, questioning attitude is deep inside the Western audience. It's important for them to think, to participate, to talk to others about the contents: what happened to us, what do we want to do, what to expect. So, theatre becomes important in the Western world because people have the chance to understand themselves by getting together and going to the theatre. A movie can be very good, but now movies are increasingly entertainment, and they're losing attraction for an audience who wants active participation. So, people tend to go back to theatre to see something more real.

AM: That's interesting because theatre then is psychologically closer to you, because you identify with it. Whereas a lot of modern films, certainly American ones, is a world you couldn't possibly be in, like science fiction, horror, action movies and so on. It's just something you watch and it's exciting, but you're not part of it. You could never be part of it. There's a bigger gap.

TY: One more question. As we know, for the past nearly 20 years China has been growing very fast. There is creativity, new technologies. World-class technologies. It seems like China is a dynamic culture now, but England is more settled and mature. So, looking at how China has been changing in these 20 years, what do you think the cultural differences will be?

AM: Well, this is what we feel in England. We feel we're living in an old country which is more or less static, that there are minor shifts, discoveries and changes, and quite rapid changes in social structure, norms and male-female relations. But we are, as Mark

Elvin describes in *The Pattern of the Chinese Past*, in a high-level equilibrium trap. We in the West are stuck in this trap now also. Certainly, what I've seen in China in the last 20 years is extraordinary. That's not your question, but most people don't know, haven't been to China and haven't studied world history. They don't realise that China has undergone in the last two generations the largest transformation – at every level, including political, but certainly social, economic, cultural – that any civilisation has ever gone through in history. It's like Japan in the 1960s-70s, except much faster and ten times the size. People in the West don't know about it, or if they knew about it, once it's happened you forget about it. But looking at it historically, if you'd said in 1978, in Deng Xiaoping times, what would China be like in 30 years, you would have imagined it would be more or less the same as it was in the previous 30 years, with a bit more. And yet, this absolutely amazing transformation of people out of poverty happened – and communications, and education, and health. And to do that calmly, with that much social tension, with far less ecological destruction than our industrial revolution caused, though it was on a smaller scale – it is miraculous. It is one of the greatest feats in human history. It's changed and transformed the world. And it's not over. Usually there are waves of transformations. The first wave was economic, technological and communications related. Now it's taking place in terms of thought, creativity, arts and so on. This is the big wave that you represent, and it is washing over us. Part of the anxiety some Western people feel about China is because they realise it's like a tsunami, vast. It's not just our restaurants and the goods we use are Chinese, but also a Chinese way of thinking, a Chinese way of perceiving, which is totally different from ours, is coming into all parts of our lives, our art, our schools, our food and everything. And so, we are feeling somewhat like the Chinese did when the British and the West came into China in the 19th century. The whole world is overflowing onto us. And so, you can either react with joy, happiness and delight in it as I do, or you can try and shut your ears and eyes and say, go away. I think there's huge potential. I've been to some of the big art galleries in Beijing, like the 798 Art Zone. I've seen your work, and it's amazing. Really amazing. Some of the work, like Ai Weiwei's, I find less interesting, though it's all interesting in different ways. Whereas if you look at our contemporary art… Well, you made a film about punk artists, *Love Infinity*. They were mildly interesting, but I didn't get a sense of greatness in any of them. And the earlier generation, Damien Hurst, Tracy Emin and so on – there's nothing.

TY: The punk artists did look interesting, and I wondered how they became like that, so I let them talk about whatever they wanted to talk about. It is true that things can fall into patterns, that economic concerns come in and change people, so they lose the content. These people don't know how to do it. They don't have the resources, and they express themselves in any way they can.

AM: In *Love Infinity*, all these interviews with those artists, Pandemonia and others... You may not want to say this, but how impressed are you by that punk art scene?

TY: The movie world now is more and more formulaic and systematised. Investment puts pressure on creative work, and there are all kinds of systems to protect the investor and the market, and that interferes too much with the creative process, I think. You can't dress a character in blue because the market doesn't like blue, so you have to replace blue with something else. Systems are terrible for creativity. Spontaneity and finding insight in the process of working is no longer possible because you have to plan and design every detail before you even start the work. I decided to make a film in a sort of primitive way and break all these rules.

I didn't care about editing and other such things. *Love Infinity* is a very personal work, and in it I allowed myself to do what I felt like doing. I wanted to see the real things. I didn't want any polishing. I deliberately set everything up in a simple, informal way. And sometimes I asked them to do something, and even I didn't know why I asked them to do it – I just shot the film. After the filming was done, I made the part with interviews and narrative. Then

I came back to the remaining chaotic footage, to see if there was meaning in the meaningless. And then it became something real. I don't know how to explain it, but among the chaos there were many moments that felt real. They were touching. And they weren't forced by any system.

AM: Do you feel that with these people?

TY: I know what you mean. I was warned not to believe anything they say because they always polish. But I say that my camera is recording their pretending, so it's real.

AM: I know nothing about art, and I know nothing about these people, but just watching it as an outsider, they seem extraordinarily provincial. They seem caught in their own time and space. If you said, there is a world out there – what about Africa or South America? what about another period of history? what about another discipline? – oh, I know nothing about that; all I know is that I wear plastic, and have plastic over my face, and feathers here; I will stick out from other people, and I will sell my artworks for huge amounts of money. Anything philosophical or historical or wider or any searching for anything... And basically, we make our money from reacting against all the traditions of the past. That's what punk is. There is no message. It's just anti-message. Just kicking other traditions. It's fun – maybe. A little bit. But it's like post-modernism. It doesn't go anywhere.

TY: Yes, but the tragic makes appearances throughout the film. It's not just about having or not having meaning or a message. I was shooting the film – the way they looked, the way they talked – whether or not it had meaning. After I collected all this together, I saw it's not something meaningless. In the film, the camera points at them, and they talk. It's not about their talking. It's how they are. I am not a tourist taking pictures of strange-looking people. I want to open the space and show how they became that way. How it happened. And what is beyond. Many people look at these artists and see that they don't look normal. But these artists believe in their way of being. Maybe there isn't much inside and everything is just on the outside with them. And yes, maybe they want to earn money. But they still believe. Someone dresses completely in plastic. Another person tattoos their whole body. They make themselves extremely far away from normal. And they want to get something. This affected me powerfully. There is no religion supporting them. Just their egos.

AM: I see…

I have another question. Through your works, we can see that you've attached great importance to spiritual strength. With advancements of technology and artificial intelligence like ChatGPT, which have almost human-like thinking, what do you think such advancement of artificial intelligence will bring to artistic creation?

TY: It's a difficult question. Nowadays, technology is developing very rapidly and even seems alive. Originally machines were invented to repeat us. Modern 'thinking machines' make our choices even more complicated. Maybe I want coffee in the morning and tea in the afternoon. But the machine would create hundreds of additional options. Maybe half coffee and half tea. The machine just calculates and produces options from its calculations. People are impressed and amazed when other human beings make discoveries from time to time. But when there is a very large number of 'discoveries' all at once, their reaction might not be as positive. There might simply be too many options.

I've talked about how human beings are losing the content, and the desire for extreme variety is an effect of that. If we live cut off from the content, we need extreme effects to feel excitement, and we are attracted by excess of excitement. Imagine, for example, that I always talk about tea. As I talk more and more, you get involved in my discourse and lose yourself because you have no space for yourself. There is only tea, tea, tea.

I have always believed in humans. Christianity talks about the soul, about a certain connection. The Japanese talk about silence. The Chinese talk about Dao. Something that includes all the moments of time. Infinity.

Artificial intelligence is what happens when whatever has been obtained by experience and thinking turns into mere data. We keep talking about things, but we no longer know why we are talking about them. Like what is happening with language. I have a critical view of words and language. When we describe something, it becomes what we describe, but not the thing itself. So, when we just know the description, all we can get is the tea-tea-tea echo chamber. It will not make us know the thing itself. But when I look at tea and experience it, I know that, okay, this is a drink. It's not just a word.

Young people talk about post-humanity these days. They are losing their identity. Losing what is human about them. The essence is being drowned in the sea of invented words. But when we are silent, we feel what is happening. There is no need to keep talking about what is happening. Take the Internet. What is it? I am not talking about technical specifications or scientific explanations now. I am talking about sensing in silence what the Internet is and why it happened in our lives.

I suggested earlier that maybe human beings came from outside of nature. Throughout human history, they have been doing something to protect themselves from nature. They searched for patterns and made calculations to adapt this unfamiliar environment to their needs. When we have new souls coming to Mars or other planets, this pattern search and calculation will happen again. The Internet is another repetition of this process. It is going through what humans went through with nature because we again found ourselves in a place we don't know and had to build the system again. But now we are finding that the system is reverting to its original state, and we are faced with moving it elsewhere. I think now is a good time to learn about origins, find that original energy and reflect on what happened in the past.

AM: When you use the word 'original', it has two meanings. Either 'original' – in other words, no one else has done it before, or the 'origin', the original state of things, the earlier state of things up to now. Which of those were you meaning?

TY: I mean why we do something in the culture.

AM: So, the origin.

TY: In a traditional culture, there is a certain spirit that moves people to symbolism. Trees or other special plants mean something. Everything in the primitive world is infused with symbolism connecting the physical and the spiritual. This symbolism develops organically; it's not a deliberate invention. It's the real content of the human spirit. I am talking about human energy coming into the world. When they entered time and space, they saw physical objects. Maybe they saw the apes. We say now that the intelligence of apes is a precursor to human intelligence. Apes have the ability to think and manipulate things around them. They can take stones and use them as tools, take something and turn it into a function for their benefit.

It's interesting to look at things and try to find where they came from, what inner structure made it happen. Some shapes are flexible and can change, but some shapes cannot change because they are original forms. That's why we look for original forms and want to know what came from them. Everything that happens in the world has an origin. When something comes from humans, we know pretty much immediately that this pattern came from humans. But when something comes from a stone, from the river, from the trees, the colours of the trees and other things we see in nature, we sense that it came from some mysterious place, from outside the logic of the physical. Much of Chinese art is about that mystery. Chinese temples have an inner energy. The roof is distinctively shaped and decorated to show that the building is related to the sky. And there are many colourful stories drawn on the walls. The building is a space for worship.

Some things go back to very early times. They are embedded deeply in the human soul. The ability to think eventually separated humans and animals. When human energy just entered time and space and encountered monkeys, this animal was unfamiliar to them to start with, but then a kind of contact and compromise happened, and the ability to think developed further and further. Religious thinking and other kinds of thinking come from there. They are not from nature, I think. Primitive forms of animism, the belief that everything is alive, is, I think, one of the first attempts of humans to understand nature and find harmony with it. Humans saw nature in a peculiar way that was relevant to themselves. They were more interested in the meaning of the sky than the ground. They were keen on understanding oceans, mountains. Things that move. And they were building protection for themselves from dangers that could be brought by living and moving parts of this nature that felt unfamiliar to them because they themselves didn't come from nature. They felt alone and afraid. This fear was the force driving the building of civilisations, I think.

AM: We're just coming to the end of the session, and I'd like to say a few words in response.

As I came to understand little bits about Chinese civilisation, I began to think of it more and more in terms of a very simple and very, very ancient set of practices and philosophies going back to three-four thousand years ago and became amazed by the way in which it had maintained continuously many features which have died away and disappeared in the rest of the world. It is a kind of container for alternatives. The most obvious one is the language; the pictographic, logographic writing system of China is unlike any other in the world on a large scale and has been maintained and will continue despite the fact that most people think that alphabetical languages are much more efficient in many ways and simpler to learn as well. But it's very ancient and it's been maintained. Then the strange Daoist/Buddhist ancestor worship kind of philosophy, which mixes up nature, culture and man, and believes that the world is filled with spirits, power, Feng Shui and so on, is extraordinary and found to a certain extent in much of south-east Asia, but in an extreme form in China and Japan. It's been maintained and it hasn't disappeared; Christian missionaries and other Westerners have not destroyed it, and the same form of quantum logic of China – both/and rather than either/or – has maintained itself. Its art system has resisted the Renaissance. So, I began to think, what an extraordinary place! It's a world on its own, like Mars or some other planet – like Japan.

I come to think all that, but what's wonderful about talking to you is that you are the first person I've met who very explicitly articulates many of these things. I know you will talk further about this, that you are interested in those links in New Orientalism and going back to those early roots, but talking to you is like talking to one of the shamans in the village I worked in, in the Himalayas, talking to someone who's got a different sense of reality but is able to bring it up and we can begin to talk about it, whereas I can talk about it with my students, but they are not as involved in all of it as explicitly as you are. It's both an enormously satisfying and mysterious experience for me which I look forward to continuing in our next conversation. Thank you very much indeed. That was wonderful.

TY: Thank you.

Lohengrin (Richard Warner) at Metropolian
and Bolshoi_Marty Sohl / Met Opera

THREE. 1 MAY 2023.

Ancient Chinese ritual vessels at Minneapolis – *Crouching Tiger* and floating above the ground – Techniques and concepts – Interpreting time and space – Killing and balance – Animation and fragmented life – European skies – The language of *Lohengrin.*

AM: Shall I start by asking one or two questions?

TY: Yes.

AM: You are doing an exhibition in Minneapolis of ancient ritual vessels. These would be totally unfamiliar to the citizens of Minneapolis or anywhere in the States or anyone in the West. Very strange. We don't have anything much like that. How do you try to make people in the West understand this kind of art?

TY: I think it's not easy because they are all studying the written information provided with the exhibits. These descriptions are based on structures, on language. They set out the facts about the objects, the data. But I find that it's possible to know, say, a spoon through such descriptions, but when I see the spoon, many more details appear, and it feels different. When I see art from the Shang dynasty and art from the Zhou dynasty, it's totally different. In the Shang dynasty they believed in all kinds of mythological animals. When people hunted, they feared the animal. And then they made the animal come out, and you can see that intense energy in the sculpture. But in the Zhou dynasty, the expression becomes more systematised. Everything becomes smaller, as if it's being described from a certain distance rather than experienced first hand and up close, like intense fear.

I think modern education is missing an important component. We are used to understanding the function of things. Function is knowledge. Knowledge has a certain process, and to know something deeply you have to enter this process. But afterwards the knowledge obtained in this way is made formulaic. The experiential part disappears. Nothing physical is left. I want to bring back the first-hand experience of knowledge. When we look at beauty and sense ourselves what feeling is being communicated, we truly understand.

I wanted to organise the exhibition as a continuous experience, a narrative, with different rooms as different chapters. You would hear sounds, you would see the light, and the light would be moving about. There would be different scenes, like a forest, a desert. In this way we would create the whole feel of the period. In the banquet scene, you would even hear the sounds of people preparing and eating food. The abstract, the sensual and the physical would be together, creating a different way to experience things. I got the chance to do it because the Minneapolis Institute of Art is a very special place. They wanted to redefine the boundaries of exhibition experience, and they totally supported the idea. And the exhibition was very well received.

AM: What is the reception? Do people who come out of the exhibition say, I suddenly understand something new about China or the world?

TY: Many, many different people came to the exhibition, from other cities and out of the state. On the opening night, many came from New York. They were very excited because this exhibition was totally different to what they usually thought of as an exhibition. They found that they were immersed in beauty. That they know more. But this 'more' is not on the level of talking. I think such immersive experiences are a good way to start using alongside formal descriptions, to connect to the beauty of things. Children love the exhibition. They play around, and they look at the exhibits with lively interest. There are many mirrors on the set, so you can see yourself all the time.

AM: Can they touch anything?

TY: No, you can't touch it.

AM: That's always the sadness of museum exhibitions. You'd like to actually feel the substance.

TY: But you can go very close. There is no description, so you look at the exhibits carefully and see them for yourself. There is no description fixing the meaning. You can see whatever you want.

AM: My next question is the same but in relation to *Crouching Tiger*. There you have the same problem. You have a mythical landscape of the traditional Qing dynasty, which is quite unfamiliar to anyone in the West. And you use all sorts of fabulous techniques of flying, fighting and so on. What was your method in trying to bring that world to a modern Western audience?

TY: I think I always understood that there are two ways. It's true that the Western world seems very different. The West has a dream of the Oriental. The Oriental is seen as something dreamlike. Like a fantasy. But I think the more refined Western taste appreciates the complex symbolism of China, details that elevate environments to another level. Floating above the ground. It's not simply a question of whether something is beautiful or not.

Crouching Tiger is about people who can float through the air. Li Mu Bai is going to the last journey of his life to become emptiness, but he cannot go all the way and comes back. I made the whole city colourless. The Qing dynasty colours are very saturated and strong. The famous 景德鎮青花瓷[6] is a representative colour in this period. Red columns in royal buildings are a signature of the time. But you don't see them in *Crouching Tiger*. I used Song dynasty colour effects: translucency, low colour, fading out. The world is fading out. And every time he sees the girl, it happens at night. Li Mu Bai's world is dark.

The imagery goes deep. You can see many wide spaces in a way that doesn't happen in other movies. A big space and two people fighting in it, in the middle of the night. It has a dream quality and is taking place on the subconscious level. The fighters are in mid-air, surrounded by space. They are like spirits, floating. This is a preparation for flying. The whole movie is a preparation for the flying scene at the end.

Li Mu Bai is a man of middle age. He is almost at the end of his

6 The famous Jingdezhen blue and white porcelain.

years of vigour, and he is facing the start of old age. He sees in the girl a reflection of his youth. There was a time when he could do anything. Now he has to be restrained and mature. It's difficult to hide things. At the end, Yu Shu Lien, Michelle Yeoh's character, sees him looking for the girl. We had a long talk about whether or not to show his intentions. In the end we decided not to show them and leave them hidden. So, his mind is hidden. And then he dies. But Shu Lien understands and accepts. Her acceptance of Mu Bai is deeply moving.

The film is a whole journey. I just saw it again after all these years. It's a really complete idea.

AM: I must see it again too.

TY: In Chinese art schools, the young generation is taught with a strong emphasis on technique. It is important that students learn good basic techniques. But in Western art education concepts are more dominant. We can see this tendency in Saint Martin's and other art schools in the West: students may not know enough technique to make the piece, but they have very avant-garde thoughts. In China they learn everything from the basics. Like oil painting, everything. How do you see the difference between these two young generations?

AM: Well, it's interesting that the West has changed so much. My grandmother was one of the first students at the Royal Academy schools in London where you were taught art. She was only 16 or 17 when she went there. I've got quite a lot of her artwork and her diaries describing what she had to do. At that time, which is about the time of the First World War, they were still using the methods developed by Sir Joshua Reynolds in the 18th century, which was exactly what the Chinese do now. In other words, you teach the techniques again and again. You put a living model or a statue and you teach the students to get it exactly right. No imagination, nothing, just copying, just being a camera, looking at this thing until their technique is absolutely perfect. And then they are qualified. That was the English-British method until the end of the First World War. Simultaneously, people like Roger Fry at King's were holding the first Impressionist exhibitions. They were holding exhibitions of Chinese art. There were parallel worlds. The students were still being taught these uncreative and copying methods, whereas art had moved on to Impressionists, post-Impressionists and so on.

And then we switched. So, I'm sure you're right, and art schools now don't spend much time on exact technique, but on creativity and so on. My grand-daughter Lily went to art college to a certain extent, and she had learned all her techniques privately by herself through years of being interested in drawing. Once she got to college, they were teaching her much more advanced things. So, now there's a big gap. I suspect that the gap will narrow because it's the same with all Chinese education. Until 10-20 years ago, most Chinese education was based on the Confucian model of heavy training in technique. You suppress imagination. You learn how the ancients did these things, so that you can replicate past wisdom. And it's only in the last generation or so that, partly through the influence of the West and other things, Chinese schools are much, much more creative. I've seen them doing art and visited a lot of Chinese schools, and the best ones now are equal to anything that we have in the West in terms of imagination and creativity.

Anyone who's thought about any art form or any academic activity knows that there are two parts. The first is, you have to learn the techniques. There are many great thinkers like Einstein, Descartes and others who say, well, school was a waste of my time, I had to break away from all that. But they forget something important. I've done a detailed study of my school, and I realised that all those boring lessons where I had to learn how to write, read, do arithmetic, learn languages – they may have been something I now don't think about and reject to a certain extent now that I have moved to a higher level. But at the time, if I hadn't got that basis, then I couldn't go to the higher level. Imagine if a pianist said, oh well, I don't need to learn how to play the piano. I will just play the piano. Instead, great pianists spend years learning technique until it becomes automatic. And so, all schools, I think, have to keep both streams. They have to to have the technique and the imaginative creative work side by side; don't go too far in either direction. I think the Chinese will probably do this extremely well, and I think our best schools are beginning to do it too.

TY: What do you think of Andy Warhol? He changed the whole way of doing art in the sixties.

AM: I've seen some of his art, and at the time it was a great shock. Now, as with a lot of later conceptual art of that time, you can't see what it's reacting against, and you can't see what is new and original about it. It was probably a necessary part of a revolution against sterility, but once you get to a stage where you throw away all the rules, you can do that only for a very short time. Then you need some new rules. Otherwise, the thing becomes chaotic. That's a very feeble answer, but that's as much as I can say.

TY: I have more questions. In 70s-80s the Western museum scene became international. There were joint art exhibitions from many nations and cultures. It was a global system, open to everyone. Diversity entered the mainstream. Now, in the 21st century, we are going towards an increasingly digital world. It is even easier to share art from another culture, and some people who are unfamiliar with the basics of that culture tend to mix various aspects of it arbitrarily. They are unaware of how and why various elements combine in the original cultural tradition. In your opinion, what are the implications of this? I think it's a big concern. How would, say, African or Mexican art need to be presented in the digital world to retain a certain sense of cultural integrity?

AM: It is, as you say, a huge change. Before it was a big effort if you wanted to know something about African or Chinese art; you either had to go there or you had to bring objects here. Now you can just press a button and there it is in front of you. That can lead to superficiality and confusion. On the other hand, one of the strange things about human beings, I think, is how quickly they can absorb unknown things. If you change it from art to food, you can take someone who's never tasted Mexican or Italian food, give them a dish to try, and even though they don't know what it's made of and its history, they can absorb it, enjoy it and feel the pleasure of it. I think this must have been the case throughout time because when, for example, during the 18th century, the great century of Chinese art coming to the West, when there was a passion for Chinese and Japanese art, most people in the West knew nothing about China. Yet, when they saw Chinese porcelain or bits of architecture, something attracted them at a subconscious level. They could see the mastery and the beauty without knowing any of the conventions, history or culture. I felt the same when I first went to China or Japan, particularly Japan. I could go into a Japanese garden, and I knew nothing – well, I didn't know anything about the history of Japanese gardens – but you sense a masterpiece somehow, in the proportions and so on. So, I think that, although there's a danger now that you just put everything together and startle people, people are getting very well trained and they're very quick. You can set up a physical exhibition or put on an online exhibition of African or Chinese art, and people will be attracted by it. And what you hope is that they will say, this is amazing, I'd like to know more about it. And then they would make the effort to go there – mentally, at least – read about it, collect other things. So, I'm fairly optimistic that we will deal with this confusion.

Right, so it's my turn to ask a question. How do you think that tradition and the future can be combined? You're working in a vast Chinese tradition, but you're also trying to imagine a future which has not yet occurred. Is this a problem in your work, combining them?

TY: I have a different way of interpreting time. Humans perceive time as a sequence of events. In that way of perception, 1960, 1970, 1980 are different times. But I think everything, whatever it is, is here all at once. The tradition is with me all the time, and the modern is with me all the time. When I focus attention on the tradition, there is tradition, and when I look at the modern, there is the modern. I open my time frame. I can move around in it, and I can mix aspects of two time periods together. It could be form, colours. Sometimes it's ideas, sometimes patterns, meaning. And there are many interactions between the different points.

There is a lot you can do with this. You can make a very surrealist reality set, which is what I do. My experience in the movies lets me play with this kind of language to communicate various things to ordinary people. If the task is to present a sad character in a film, I would change the colours, I would arrange the room differently, with or without a window. It's like a language, but it's on the subconscious level. Even though there is no script, putting certain things in certain places, certain arrangements, connect to people's internal perceptions of the visual and convey emotion through that.

That is what I do in movies. I try to understand what is now, what are we facing, what does the environment mean to us, and what possibilities there are. I want to put it like a mirror, to look at the whole world. When you want to know the world, you just take a grain of sand because the whole world is reflected in that grain of sand. So, when I am working on a movie set in the Song dynasty, I prepare a very detailed representation of the Song dynasty. We have to imagine all the props and all the details to be shown to the audience. It is different from scientists or museum people. They have to have facts and proofs, otherwise they cannot say anything. But I am making a movie, and I can't put just one cup in the set because that is the only thing validated by facts. We have to fill in many blanks, and where there is no proof or evidence, we have to create, though this creation is done consistently with what is known about that historical period.

I also have to deal with the creative vision of the director, so that when I am putting the scene together, I have to think about camera movement. When I worked with John Woo, I made many moving props and left more space in the room, so that he can put in the dolly to do the shooting. But in Tsai Ming-Liang's lens, he, the director, was shooting the reality environment of the actor, and the real life did the whole thing itself. I didn't even touch anything. He just put in the angle, a wide angle. Because in his mind, the language *is* shooting the real thing. It's a choice, like photography. He didn't create things; he just put the angle. Ang Lee is different in his own way. Every director has a different language. I feel free to go into certain people's minds to see how they express things, how they use their vocabulary, how they use movement, how they use the emotional exchange with the audience. I need to understand that in order to know how to frame it to make all these things visible and accessible. That's what my work is about. So, in movies, there is a lot of this kind of mixing of different times and concepts. Many things happen in one second when we're thinking about the set and thinking about how the story goes.

AM: Interesting. My question suggested a distinction between tradition, the present and then the future, but you don't make any distinction between tradition and the present.

TY: Actually, it's complicated. When we are working on a culture from a very long time ago, and not much information is known about this early tradition, we have to guess. And we might take another similar period of time and see whether material about that time period could be adapted and used to build up a believable image of the time period we are working on. It's tentative, of course. But with the Qing dynasty, for example, a lot of detail is known, and these details are known to the audience too, so we have to be accurate and consistent when building the sets.

After that, you build up your artistic language. This is different. Nowadays it's complicated because we don't have a definition of what it is we're looking at. We open our eyes and look outside, and many different time periods are overlapping right there, in front of our eyes. There might be an old building, say several hundred years old. And on that building, there might be a very modern-looking sign. We look at people in the street: someone is dressed fashionably, while another wears old-style clothes. Some cars are very old, some are brand new. Different times are all mixed together. Everything is overlapping, overlapping, overlapping. Even the weather. Maybe a hundred years ago the weather was a little bit different, but we can't tell because such things seem the same and change only very slowly. There are so many things evolving, overlapping and mixing, and we can see so many things at the same time.

AM: Complex world you are living in… My next question is, how did you manage to move from sketching to photography to working with film? They seem to use totally different techniques.

TY: I was always drawing, from a very young age. Maybe I liked drawing because these were the only tools available to me at the time. My elder brother was a photographer, and he had a beautiful camera.

AM: What age were you when you got your first camera?

TY: A teenager. I was always following my brother around. He had very good equipment, and I used his equipment to take photos everywhere. So, I started to understand photography. My brother was a portrait photographer. He was always shooting people. He taught me that you have to see their eyes. But that's because he was working in a commercial environment where you have to control the effects. If you are doing something commercial, you have to control the message. It's different from catching a moment on the camera. You have to direct the object to be in a specific way. Later I started to shoot when they called me, and I did not direct or manipulate the object.

My brother's assistant was working in movies. He knew that I could draw, and he asked me to help him to do a movie set. Set painting. I painted the whole wall. After that more and more people found out that I did that kind of work and asked me to work as an art direction assistant. The first movie I worked on was *A Better Tomorrow* by John Woo. It's a very famous movie.

AM: What year was that?

TY: 1986.

AM: You were quite young.

TY: Yes, really young. I just started the journey.

AM: When you say you started – did you do any filming at that stage?

TY: I did art direction. Set decoration. And I continued doing photography too. There was a magazine at that time, the only magazine about movies in Hong Kong. Everyone read that magazine. I took photographs for it, of actors and also the behind-the-scenes people. Every issue had my work in it. People knew me as a photographer and journalist at that point. Afterwards I did another movie: *Rouge*, directed by Stanley Kwan. It's set in 1930s in Hong Kong. There are courtesans and all kinds of colourful people in it. I started learning more and more to understand how to build up the time period in which the film's action takes place.

AM: But have you actually *made* a film? I mean, held the camera and made a whole film?

TY: Oh, that's much later, when Lili came along, and I wanted to make a movie. I was also invited to do a short movie with Chanel in Paris, with participation of famous actors and actresses.

AM: And you held the camera?

TY: Yes. I held the camera and directed.

I would like to learn something about your childhood in India. How your world started and how your world changed in that period of time. And how it contributed to your later views.

AM: I was born in 1941 in Assam, on the border of Burma and China. Although I can't remember any of it, I know that most of what I am now was formed in those first four or five years when I was in Assam. My mother kept a little book – the English had them; I don't know if the Chinese have this – this one was called the 'Babees Book', with 'ees'. I still have it. The mother would put in: baby was born today, and the people who were there were so and so. Then a week or a month or two months later: the baby stood up and said their first word or whatever it is. So, I have little snapshots. My mother and father were apart, so my mother was writing to my father who was in the army. This was during the war. She would write saying, Alan is doing this and doing that, and he's very good, or very bad, or whatever it was. Because of this, I have an unusual account of my infancy which I put into the first volume of my autobiography. So, I have little senses and I have quite a lot of photographs. And I can see little bits of the influence. One was that I was ill a lot; because it's India, and I nearly died of various stomach things and so on. That has affected my health a little bit throughout my life. I can also see that my mother was progressive in encouraging my friendships. There weren't many white children there, and my best friend, she tells me – and I've got photographs of him – was a little Indian boy. I learned the native language of ordinary Indians. We weren't on a tea plantation yet, so my life was really Indian because my *ayah*, the person who looked after me in the daytime a lot, and my best friends, and all the landscape, were Indian. I was in this strange half-and-half world, which doesn't exist now so much because the British Empire has gone, where you are in the top 1% of the British running this huge country, but you're also part of the deeper, mythical and feeling world of India. Luckily, I don't have to describe it because it's been described by one of our greatest writers, Rudyard Kipling. All you have to do, if you want to understand my childhood, is to read *The Jungle Book*. I was Mowgli. My friends were not exactly bears, but it was that world of talking animals, adventures, of never knowing when the snake would come. I think the fact that I got stuck directly in one academic discipline, that I wanted to go and become an anthropologist, travel to China and so on, is because very early on I lived in a much richer kind of feeling and other world than I would have done if I'd been brought up in an English village. Like Kipling, whose great works are autobiographical and about his childhood, really – *The Jungle Book*, *Kim* and others – although he left India quite early. So, it's had an immense influence, and I'm enormously grateful for the chance to have experienced the last days of the British Empire. I should be ashamed of it, but I wasn't responsible at the time.

TY: I am very interested in how you became an anthropologist. I feel that because you have had oriental influence in your life, you see in different ways and get deeper insights. That's why I want to know your background, how you grew up and how you found yourself to be here.

AM: Well, as I've probably mentioned, I know myself better than almost anyone in the world. I've written, I'm now counting them up, around 30 volumes of my autobiography, including my ancestors. I'm just finishing the 29th volume. It's a longer account of how someone grew up, through to the present time than anyone has ever attempted in their lives. And there are one or two volumes about anthropology. Anthropology is not a discipline. It's not like history or mathematics or chemistry or geography. It's not something you do; it's something you are. It's the same as being an artist or a musician. In other words, you don't start your anthropology at 9 o'clock in the morning and end it at 6 in the evening. Your whole life, you become an anthropologist. All the time it's influencing you. In some ways I'm not a very good anthropologist. My wife is a better anthropologist than I am. Because she is, as many women are, more sociable, more interested in other people. So, when we are on a bus, she is the one who is talking to people; I'm just sitting, thinking. I'm not the kind of anthropologist who goes around, stops people in the street and starts talking to them. On the other hand, my anthropology is of a school that is basic to early anthropology, which is trying to understand the whole world – and every aspect of the world. The thing that really appeals to me about anthropology is that in our modern world we split our lives off. So, we have our economic area where we make money and think about wealth. Then we have another area, politics, where we are involved with power. We have another area, which is religion and thought. And another area, which is our social life. Now anthropologists went to societies like China, where you don't split these spheres of life, where music is not just making of sounds and artworks are not just artworks – they are part of an unbroken, seamless web of symbolic and other associations. When I went to Nepal to do my fieldwork in a small Himalayan village, I went to a world where you couldn't separate anything. If someone gave someone a gift – this is a famous example in anthropology – it's a symbolic object, it's everything, all connected. So, when I gave you this biscuit in Nepal, it's not just a biscuit. It's a social relation. There is what they call *hau* in one language: the gift has spirit, so if I gave you a gift, you have to give me a gift back because you now have the spirit.

I became an anthropologist, I think, partly because of the Indian background, but also after having studied history for six years at university, I began to be dissatisfied because historians took these separations for granted. If I had stayed in history, I would have become a specialist on economic history in a particular century, in a particular country – terribly narrow. My questions have always been the huge questions. Why are we as we are? What are human beings? What unites us across the world? What differentiates us? I want to know about the whole of human history from the first hunters and gatherers to the present, and about every different civilisation and how it works. Historians don't do that, so I had to become an anthropologist. It's a wonderful discipline because whatever you do, someone says, 'Alan, why are you going off to do that in… somewhere?' And I say, well, it's anthropology – because it's impossible to think of any subject which is not anthropology. What you and I are doing now when we talk is anthropology. As is going anywhere, studying anything. I could write a hell of a thesis on Lili. This is a wonderful anthropological subject, Lili. Anthropology empowers you to connect, and connecting different parts of things is what anthropologists do.

TY: This is amazing because anthropologists describe humans in different ways and change the perception, the ways we look at human beings. The question of knowledge and language is interesting. Language alters the way humans look at the world; it imposes itself. In Eastern cultures, they always think about the space. They are not talking about themselves, but about the space, and they try to understand the space. They make a balance. Just as you said when we were talking about eating, in early times we killed animals and ate them. But in so many different religions there was expressed a need to give something back to the animals to restore the balance. It's not the same with language. When we use words, 'I need to eat, so I take this animal', the animal itself becomes different. Our speaking is complete, but the world is left incomplete, in a state of imbalance. I think balance is a way to make things harmonious. But it's difficult. Nature itself is not always harmonious. It creates disasters too.

AM: This is why I'm particularly interested in China. It restores the balance to a larger extent. It's a balanced civilisation where you haven't made the breaks and separations which we've made in the West. These separations are needed to create a certain kind of science and technology: you need to separate things and use the Cartesian methods and so on. But it has also led to disasters. Unless we rebalance with a more integrated vision of our connectedness to nature, to the world and to other human beings, our world will blow itself up. So, this is what interests me.

The last thing I'd like to say is that when you're talking about language, many people say, well, you think you can write books about Japan and China, and you don't speak a word of the language – how can you possibly do that? And that does go against anthropology: usually, you do learn the language. On the other hand, I've found that communicating with a special person like you or some of the friends I've made in China and Japan and elsewhere, it is possible to get beyond language because there are many things one can't express in language. But through friendship and through effort, you can get to another level, rise above language, and learn deeper things about another civilisation, which you wouldn't learn if you just learned the language and tried to use that.

TY: I think language has been used to construct conceptual structures in human societies. Perhaps in earlier times it was not such a problem because the population wasn't very large. One million people is one thing, but when you have ten billion people, systems have to change. Very many details appear. …I'm always talking about something and then flying off in another direction. You don't have this problem, right?

AM: Well, that's a suggestion that we need lunch. We'll stop there, have some lunch and continue after.

*

AM: So many questions… What do you think about the relationship between technology and art?

TY: I think technology is very important. As you've mentioned earlier, it's the tools, the language of what you're thinking. Art is the thinking, and technology is the language.

AM: You've used many different media in your work. Two that I don't know that you've used are sculpture and animation. Have you ever experimented with those, or are you intending to do so?

TY: I did quite a lot of sculpture and love it. In 2008 I was setting up a contemporary art exhibition, and my curator asked me to do something that I haven't done before. I chose sculpture. It just came into my mind. I love sculpture because it's like building up something physical from emptiness. I go deeply into the rhythms of the shapes and the lines and the relationship of different lines. It can be complicated, and the energy form will be really strong. I'm using my body to feel the sculpture. Different materials give me different force. It's about the reaction of the force and the reaction of the line to build up the force. When you're looking at a sculpture, you're moving. You are walking around it, seeing it from different angles and at different distances. The scale will be different too, related to your human body. Sculpture is always a physical thing that relates to the viewer's body, so that they can feel it. I really like sculpture.

As for animation… I take a lot of photographs. Most of the time it happens when I see something that produces a reaction within me. I feel the message, and I take the photographs. The image has a kind of energy, the energy has a kind of message. I borrow the experience I have when I'm taking photographs and take it into my other works. And I understand it that way. In the past five years especially, short animation became very popular. I think it's an extension of photography. It's not photography, and it's not a movie – it's in the middle. It's like a hybrid of image and movement. I find that it makes a strong impression on me. It's something to represent time now, because everything becomes fragmented, everything becomes a feeling in the short term. Easy to understand, easy to touch, no content. These kinds of things become a kind of narrative of nowadays, mostly for the young generation. This affects music, art, it affects the understanding of things. I believe that this will bring us to another way of mixing time and elements. In my generation we think we have a linear kind of understanding of the world, but the new generation doesn't have that inner line. All they have is fragments. So, it's good for me to understand this way of expression, the narrative of the young generation. To connect with the next generation, to understand their language, we need to learn this way of fragmented expression.

AM: I know you've been influenced by Japanese animation, anime, Miyazaki and people like that. If you get onto Japanese underground, you see them all reading comics – and animations are very, very strong in Japanese aesthetics. Have you any idea, any theory about why?

TY: I think the Japanese are always living in their mind. Physically they live in very small spaces, pressing themselves to be more and more compact. Earlier there were big companies, and people working for such companies were under much stress but also felt protected to an extent. This has ended, and people feel unprotected and afloat now. The 80s was a very rich time for Japan. It was a special time for the Japanese spirit, and economically Japan was perhaps the second biggest economy then.

I think Japanese history also made a deep impact. I read Akira Kurosawa, and he talked about how the bomb affected Japan. There was a sense of urgency to create before everything disappeared. This feeling propelled a lot of artistic expression into existence. There are also many novels talking about the old times and the new. I worked a lot on novels. There is a sense of small islands – beautiful flowers growing in small patches, the scenery changing fast. Even the ground is uncertain when there are so many earthquakes. The tendency becomes to concentrate on small details of the fleeting beauty, as if they want to hold on to the moment of time that is quickly disappearing.

Japanese relationship with space is also very interesting. I think it came from China a long time ago. The Japanese kept it and absorbed it deeply into their culture. The Japanese are always doing that. They are good at absorbing powerful cultures and making them organically their own. Japan has a lot of imagination, a lot of passion. There are many themes of destruction, scenarios where the whole world is destroyed, like Akira. But this creates a lot of energy. Young energy. They don't understand, they don't control anything, they don't know the future, but they just want to try something. They see the whole world is upside down, and they try to find a way. This is very attractive to the rebels, the young generation. Because the young generation feels, we have nothing, we struggle against everything surrounding us, including the previous generations, and we want to build something of our own. This kind of energy is becoming very powerful in attracting the young generation.

How do you feel about China? I know that you have a deep relationship with Chinese culture. And many contacts. What aspects of Chinese character and culture you find most memorable?

AM: Well, to explain how I feel about China would take a long time. I only discovered China very late in my life. I went there first when I was about 55, and I've been particularly interested since I was 65-67. I sometimes wonder whether I wish I had met China earlier, but in a way, it's nice to have one of the crowning experiences of your life late in life. And also, I've always thought that I only understood Japan because I came from Nepal, which is a similar sort of shamanic world, and I think I understand China better because I came to thinking about and experiencing China after trying to understand Japan. I think if I hadn't understood Japan quite well by the time I came to China, China would be even more strange. But there's enough overlap, particularly in the arts and culture, to make it half-familiar. There are a million things that I love about China. I like Chinese food. I like the Chinese landscape, which is very beautiful.

If I had to pick out, I would select two things.

The first would be the Chinese people, whom, I think I may have said before, I find immensely attractive, interesting, warm, resourceful. I just like the people, enjoy being with the Chinese and going back to China.

The second thing is hope. I think the West, its philosophy and its way of life have dominated the world for the past couple of centuries, and it has produced many marvels in science and arts. But it needs refreshing, and China can refresh it and give it a new impetus. In terms of international politics, I'm deeply worried by the Western confrontational and aggressive approach, what they call 'zero-sum game'. In other words, it's the 'if you gain, we lose' mentality of my part of the world, the Anglosphere (the English and the Americans). We just about survived 500 years spent in imperial aggression, bullying and fighting because we didn't have nuclear weapons and weren't interlocked in the way that we are now. The world has changed; we *have* those things. And if we continue in that kind of binary philosophy, 'I'm right, you're wrong', good and evil, then we as a race won't last for many more years. China is based on Confucian, Daoist and other philosophies, and even the popular Chinese game Go is one where you surround the other players, not kill them. In China it has traditionally been taught, even in *The Art of War*, that you don't fight the battle by killing people, you fight the battle by getting yourself in a position where they have to surrender. Chinese philosophy and the nature of its empire, civilisation and history provides an alternative which, I think, is much more suited to an international world of the kind we have now. So, I'm hoping that China will quickly spread its influence, as it's already doing in the Middle East with the recent treaty between Iran and Saudi Arabia, and as it's trying to do with Russia and Ukraine, as well as with Palestine and Israel. Its goal is peace and mediation, whereas the goal of America and Britain, to a large extent, seems to be to create more work for the arms industry and cause more fighting. That's how we've succeeded for 500 years.

China gives me hope. There are many things one can criticise in China, like everywhere else, but when young people ask me, have you got hope about the future, I say, yes, I've got several things, and one of them is China. As China becomes more influential, it is, on the whole, a force for good. I'm not frightened of it.

Those are the two things I like most about China: the people and the hope it produces.

TY: That's wonderful.

In the period when you were developing your theories and accumulating knowledge, what did you think about the evolution of the world? How did you understand the world globally then, and how did your views change since?

AM: I started in a very, very narrow way because I was trained as a historian, and the only thing I learned about was England, a little bit of Europe, and nothing about the rest of the world. Likewise, when I started as an anthropologist, I looked at one little village, one little community. Gradually, as I may have said elsewhere, I felt my life become like climbing a mountain: the views became wider, and I could see more from above. So, in some ways, alongside seeing further and wider, things became simpler. For many people, as they grow older, the world becomes more confused and more difficult to understand. I've been fortunate through my work, working out certain principles which make the world quite simple to understand. I'm a very, very small mind and a small body living now, but there have been a number of great minds in the past, and so I've written a series of books about five or six great thinkers, like Montesquieu, Tocqueville, Adam Smith, one Japanese, Fukuzawa, and I have, as we say, climbed on these giants' shoulders. Just here, on my own, I can only see a little bit. The great thing about those five or six thinkers is that they spent their whole life thinking, and then usually they put it into one or two books like *The Wealth of Nations* or *The Spirit of the Laws*. They did it by reducing complexity to simplicity, and then they created some principles, tendencies or structural features, and so I've looked at those, brought them together, and with such a toolkit of simple structural features, I can now go to somewhere like China. Whereas my colleagues who study China might say, oh, Alan, you can't understand China, you know nothing about it, etc. – but when I talk to them, I realise they don't know anything about China because the complexity confuses them, whereas I look at China through the eyes of Tocqueville or Montesquieu, and it's actually a very simple structure anthropologically. And then, if I can have that structure here, then I can look at the structure of Europe or the structure of India and compare them. Gradually the confusions that are caused by too much data begin to disappear, and you can see things more clearly. You can see right down – I've probably used this metaphor with you before, but basically, it's like looking into a rushing river and then suddenly everything clears, and you can see the bottom, every little pebble. Once you have that, when I go back to China, as I hope to in October, I won't have to start all over again and be confused by finding this or that. I will have a broad picture and then be able to fit this new experience and this new conversation with you into it. I'm learning a huge amount from talking to you, and it's fitting in with things that I roughly know – and now know a little bit better. My life has really been simplifying and rising up. My turn to ask a question. You've travelled a lot in your life. Where did you go in your early travels?

TY: I've been to many different places, but most of my travel happened in my early twenties, when I went to Europe. I just took my bag and went by myself, on a very limited budget. Sleeping in trains and things like that.

AM: Around Europe?

TY: Yes. I wanted to find out why I liked European art. What I saw of European and American art in Hong Kong was very limited. There were a lot of big things going on in the art world of that period, and I wanted to experience all this first hand, so I went to Europe. It was amazing. This trip had a profound influence on me because when I saw European art, I reacted to it on a deep level. I felt that this art was coming from within myself. It felt very familiar, like coming back to a world I already knew. I felt a connection with the artists who created that art. It's as if I knew what they were thinking and feeling. I could sense the very way they touched the canvas with the brush. It all felt closely related to my inner self. I got a lot of experience during that trip, and the works of art I saw then still return to my mind today and are instrumental in my creative experimentation.

AM: Apart from the inspiration of the art, were there any features of other parts of life in Europe that influenced you later on?

TY: I think romance is very important. We went to Paris and the south of Italy, places famous for the romantic experience. It is born from the land, I think, and the music, the wine and everything. You feel really relaxed. In Hong Kong, it's not easy to feel that kind of relaxation, though Hong Kong has a lot of places that are very good for holidays and relaxing. Very elegant places too. But you just don't feel the same kind of relaxation when you're in Hong Kong. In Europe, you feel it in a different way. You go to a farm to have dinner and drink wine for four hours. There is no time limit. I could stay there for a long time, and there were beautiful scenes everywhere. I agree that this is a projection, but it is also a reality.

Before I saw Europe, I used to look at the colour of the sky and the trees in some of the European paintings and wonder how the artists felt these things and created those colours. But when I went to Europe, I saw that the real thing is the same as the painting. They just copied it. They are still beautiful, those colours they saw. It's almost like a dream. In Europe, there are no earthquakes, no storms. It's like a gift from the gods.

AM: That's why I wanted to take you round a little bit of England, so you can see it's a bit like that too.

Which of the great directors and artists you've worked with have influenced you most and you've been most impressed by?

TY: I think many of them. Everyone gives me a different world. I mainly cooperate with directors like Robert Wilson. Akram Khan. Ang Lee, of course. John Woo. It's really powerful. They each have their own world. When I work with them, I feel welcome to enter into their worlds, and they're open to giving me information. I try to support the vision they are creating and contribute to it. It's like a gift.

AM: How do you get to know them? Does it take a long time, or do you just immediately start talking about art and communication?

TY: It depends. In the movies you will get closer to the person's inner world. The emotional world. You have to catch that kind of mystery. It's not open. It's very private. You have to touch an innermost part and express it in a movie, and you have to take care of all kinds of creative elements. But in theatre, it seems more general, so that we talk about concepts and other things. In movies, I work more on the psychological side. In theatre, it's more about form, or language. I have very good experience working with Akram Khan. We started talking almost at first sight, and we felt connected. And then we worked on many, many projects together, and developed the language.

AM: Have you ever argued with anyone? You seem such a friendly and easy person. I can't imagine you having a fierce argument with any director or artist, but have you done that?

TY: I try not to, because as I'm working, I'm gauging how I can contribute. What is in the director's mind? Maybe there is something he doesn't have that I might have, in which case I make a suggestion. When he says yes, I know that he found it useful. It's not like I want to impose Tim Yip on his film. I'm open. Tim is like a supermarket. I will give suggestions only when they are needed. Even in this way of working, when the film comes out, the style of my work is immediately recognised.

When I'm beginning a film, I'm excited to know something outside of me. I don't want to be just going in circles within myself. I want to have another's input, because I work with them, and they have something that I don't have. I want an exchange. Like ping-pong. I don't know what the film will come out to look like, because we're finding this out in the process. And then when we find it in the process, the director is the one who is creating it, so we don't have an argument. If I have my idea that I want red, and he wants white, that cannot be reconciled. But when I sense, oh, he is saying white now, but he wants red, I tell him, oh, red can come in later. And throughout the film, red does slowly come in, and he feels, wow, you really know me. Then that will make the deal. I think I have a hard time when the director is not serious about work. When he's not putting himself into the work, so he'd be suddenly changing this or that.

AM: What do you do when you find people who are not really serious about the work? Do you let the interaction fade away, or do you continue to try and work with them?

TY: It depends. Sometimes I walk away in my own way, and sometimes I try to change things.

AM: Your answers were quite short, so I'll ask you a third question. You're working on Wagner's *Lohengrin*. I don't know if it's finished, but you've been working on it recently. Opera is a relatively new art form for you, and Wagner's pretty difficult. What are the main challenges in working on that?

TY: The big challenge is that it's a big production in America. I think it's the biggest scale of production in the opera world, so I need to have a very strong idea, the support of the director, of course, to create a new language of opera.

My intention is to introduce abstract language into opera. Rather than building on the dramatic development of the story, historical references, opera conventions or theatre conventions and separating the language, I want to try to create an abstract language of colours based directly on Wagner's music. Earlier I did *Tristan and Isolde*, and the music separates them into two different characters, so I wanted to take that and turn it into visuals. We create a world ravaged by war, where everyone is living underground. It's as if everybody is dying, but they are still fighting between themselves. It's a deeply tragic world. Gods are portrayed as cold and unmerciful. Wagner was already bringing up the relationship between gods and people. Gods are not always friendly. They can be fierce and demanding. All this is conveyed through music and becomes abstract. Wagner's music is intensely emotional, even when it is high-key, like a military celebration. Wagner created a special world at a special moment in time, as Nietzsche was working out his philosophies. He expressed the whole atmosphere of that time in music, including the heightened state of emotional intensity.

That's what I am doing too. The destroyed, dying world and its sick and dirty underground inhabitants are represented by grey, and then the grey is replaced by bright colours. It's an abstract idea, but I am very interested in it, and I think it's been successful. People understand it, and that makes me satisfied with the work.

They all come from music, and even the conductor likes it a lot.

AM: We're coming towards the end, but I think we've still got a couple of questions.

TY: I think the book you wrote for your grand-daughter Lily is very interesting. It talks about many things. I think it's a little bit overwhelming for a little girl, but it's really interesting. It's like a bible before you come into the complicated real world. But a silly question is, how did you expect to get all this information to Lily?

AM: Well, I spent much of my life writing academic books, and one of my very close friends who wasn't an academic said, Alan, can't you write a simple book for ordinary people that summarises all that you've learned? I was about 60, and I had a beautiful grand-daughter Lily whom I absolutely adored. We spent a lot of time in child's games and worlds together.

TY: How old was she?

AM: She was about seven or eight when I wrote it for her, but I imagined she would be about 16 or 17. When I was 16 or 17, going from adolescence to maturity, I had many questions about very broad things: the meaning of life and why this happened and who was God and things like that. I never asked people, because I knew that adults would say, well, we can't answer those now, wait when you've grown up.

This is what happened to Einstein. Einstein explained why he was great. He said, when I was a child, I asked big questions about things like space and time and the meaning of life. And everyone said, oh, you know, can't answer those questions now, wait till you're grown up. And he said, other people asked these questions too, but when they grew up, they forgot the questions, but I went on asking the simple questions of childhood when I grew up.

So, I thought, if I were a 16-17-year-old girl going into this present world, what would I like an adult to tell me? I knew that if she went to a teacher and said, tell me about terrorism, tell me about bureaucracy, tell me about war, tell me how my family system works, they'd say, well, wait till you're grown up, because they didn't know. They weren't trained anthropologists. People don't know their own system.

I sat down and placed her in front of me – because you have to do that when you're writing; you have an audience, and you place someone. I didn't have an actual Lily, but in my mind, I put Lily there. Each letter started with 'Dear Lily'. For example... 'Dear Lily, you must have been thinking about your feeling about God. Does he exist or doesn't he exist? Because if he exists, then he must be a terrible person, because look what he's created. If he doesn't exist, then the world is meaningless and there's no point to it, so what am I to do?' I then explained to her about God. I wrote the letters very quickly, some of them in Japan, but it only took me six months or so. I'd just sit and write for a couple of days, and there was this one on beauty or whatever it was. I published it. All I did with her at that point was to get her to read through the titles. I said, can you understand the question? What is war? What is justice? And she said, yes, I can understand the question.

I didn't get her to read the answer, but she read two of the letters and made a delightful sort of very perceptive errors. One of them was, she asked, what is *demo crazy*? We in the West now think democracy is crazy; we have Donald Trump. The next one she looked at and said, what is *bureau crazy*? And we think bureaucracy is crazy too. That was enough. I said, Lily, when you're a little older, you will read this. I gave the book to her when she was about 12 or 13, because quite a lot of my friends have children, and they give it to their children from about 12 or 13. And girls particularly: very, very clever. Some of them read it at 12 or 13 and liked it. Anyway, I asked her at 12 or 13 how she was getting on with it. And she's very sensitive; she knew I wanted her to say 'I love it' or 'I've read it carefully' or something. But she's also very honest. And so she said, actually, Baya, which is what she calls me, I couldn't read beyond the first page – I've only read one page. I said, why? What's wrong with it? She said, well, there are three things about a good book, and it hasn't got any of them. No pictures. No animals. No story. Useless!

Being me and obstinate, I said, OK, let's rewrite it. I said to Lily, how about you and I write it together with animals, story and pictures? So, I wrote a little book, which I just self-published, called *The Batipedia*. It was a Wikipedia written for bats. I retell the stories, but with animals in it. Lily and I going for adventures within a world of bats: different kinds of bats, bats falling in love, terrorist bats, bureaucratic bats. We had adventures with all these things, and she did the pictures at the beginning. She read it carefully, corrected some of my grammar and so on. So, that is the one for 11-12-year-olds.

It was a kind of liberation for me because throughout my life I've done two doctorates and written many academic works, and in all of them I've worked out the argument of my books very, very carefully: each paragraph, lots and lots of data, lots of materials to support it, lots of footnotes – typical academic books. And this book... actually it was the second, but it was the extreme example of something where I just sat down with a sheet of paper and said, today I'm going to write on our legal system or whatever the question was. I just wrote and then the next day I glanced at it and continued writing; after a couple of days, I looked at it again and typed it out. Free writing – it liberated me. I moved from technique to the imaginative level. That was 2002. In the last 20 years I have written about 40-50 books like that. Just from inside and not from the head. And so, I owe a huge amount to my Lily, just as you do to your Lili.

On that happy note, thank you again for a lovely talk. And I look forward to our next – soon, I hope.

TY: Something you said struck a chord in me. It's about another world besides the physical world. We always dream about this world and feel that it exists, but it's impossible to describe it.

AM: Parallel worlds. I've got that question for you later.

Mirroring Coexistence Fake and Real ©Tim Yip Studio

Four. 10 May 2023.

Expanding perception – Moving out of time and back in – Patterns – Existing and not existing – Art as transmission of energy – Chinese Buddhism and Daoism – What is freedom? – What is fake? What isn't fake? – Zen and Dao – It's time to balance.

AM: It's a great pleasure to see you again. I very much look forward to these meetings. Thinking about what we've been talking about and our exploration, I don't know about you, but for me it's extremely helpful and valuable. It's very difficult for a European to get inside the culture of China and it needs someone you can trust and someone who you have established a bond with. So, I feel that I am on a very exciting journey with you.

(turning towards Lili) Hello, Lili. Nice to see you. Welcome again.

I'll start with a big one: what are your biggest dreams and your goals in future artwork? What do you hope to do?

TY: Human beings, when they came into this time and space, opened a window between time and space and another place, but I don't know where it is. This isn't limited by body or age. The gift of being a human being is the ability to pass back and forth through that window, between infinity and the world of physical things. It's a mysterious ability. We can move to infinity and from there see ourselves. When I go deeply into Chinese culture, I see that they were looking for that. Ancient sources talk about practising to control your mind. In the West, people talk about freeing your mind, but it's the same thing. By controlling the Chinese don't mean making the mind tense, they mean developing the ability to focus. When there is the ability to focus intensely, we perceive in a way that isn't intellectual knowledge, and it's not possible to put this level of perception into the mundane language of facts and data. It doesn't matter what is being looked at, what matters is the level of perception of the one who is looking. Our power is to understand without talking, by perceiving and exploring for ourselves. This wordless knowing can take the form of mirroring. For example, I could look at trees and from their lines sense whether or not they are healthy. Or stroke a dog and know by mirroring what's happening to the dog. From this perspective, it's interesting to look at the human world afresh. For example, why did humans make this cup? How did they choose these grapes? How many tests did they make to decide which tastes suited them and which didn't? It's a way to see through everything. As you said last time, the Chinese are focussed on relationships. We don't start from our point of view of looking at something – we start with the space. So, the space is looking back at us, and in it there is a deep togetherness of everything. So, when you cut a tree, you have to plant another, so as not to disturb the togetherness. Carelessly turning a tree into a chair leaves an imbalance in the wholeness of things. Balance is everywhere. Waters come down as rain, get absorbed, then evaporate, and the circle starts again. The paths of rebalancing differ, but the balance is still attained. Just like when I'm drawing the spiritual DNA drawings, I always know from within where to start and where to finish. The finish is where the balance is attained. I draw a line; then I draw another to balance it, but the balance is not yet complete; so, I draw another line, and another – as many as are needed to make the drawing balanced. Then the drawing is complete, and I stop. I think calligraphy in China is also this way. Sometimes they want to break the balance and sometimes they keep the balance. Balance is calming, and in the state of balance our perceptive abilities are at their best.

AM: That's very interesting… When you said you were trying to explore things beyond knowledge, it reminded me of a recent talk I went on by a cosmologist, someone trying to study the origins of the universe. He stressed, as we now know, that we only understand 5% of what is in the universe. We understand the 5% that is matter. Dark matter, which is another 20%, we don't even know whether it's matter. We don't know what it is. Dark energy, which is 75%, we just know it must be there, but we don't know what it is. So, in a way, what you are trying to do is to explore dark matter and dark energy, things which are beyond current knowledge and going down deeper. They must be there because physicists see their effects, but they can't explore them directly and they have not devised any scientific tests for finding out what dark matter or dark energy is. So, we have to use other methods than usual methods to discover it.

TY: Yes. I think there is no such thing as dark matter. Everything is the same. Neither dark matter nor ordinary matter are matter for the universe. It's just a way of balancing. When we start thinking about dark matter, a separation arises between what is dark matter and what is ordinary matter, and our view becomes limited. Dark matter and ordinary matter are contained in one another, or they are reflections of one another. Neither could exist otherwise. We need to set aside terms like dark matter and look at what is happening. It's like with black holes. I think these too are a reflection and rebalancing of energy. We should look at what's happening underneath. For example, if I think you are very good and I like you, my face and behaviour would show it, but most importantly my heart, the way I feel within. When you see my face and my behaviour, you can feel that I like you. You look at appearances, but you notice the important thing underneath these appearances. I think the material world arose because energy crystallised and turned into what we call matter. Everything that exists in time and space is dead. It has no life of its own but can appear alive because it replenishes energy from outside of itself. Take the human body, for example. It is dying every moment and is replenished with energy every moment. When you are looking at me, I am still alive and moving. But only for a very short moment. It's not real existence. I appear alive because I constantly replenish my energy. A human life in space and time is like that. A very strong energy puts a child into space and time, and they are 'alive' for a certain period. A child's energy is very strong because they open the space for energy to come in. They are pure and not afraid of anything. But as they know more and more, they become limited and worried, which makes them weak. The drop in incoming energy weakens the physical body as well. But the tricky thing is, every moment is the same. The very young and the very old know that because every moment is individual, you can refresh yourself at any time, and all this is just a concept. When you are open, suddenly everything changes. This is something that is not in the logic, it is not in the knowledge, but you can feel it sometimes. And you can sort of practise getting better at it. When you are doing things involving memory, it's very good to open yourself, and this alternating, get information and open, get information and open, makes perception more and more accurate. I think everything is about energy and energy looking for balance. So, black holes could be energy that's losing its circulation power. It will be undefined and go to infinity again. As energy concentrates into matter, there appear small islands of matter in a large environment of circulating energy. These small islands of matter grab energy from outside. I think modern science is in the period of trying to understand matter. When we understand matter and are then able to look at the bigger picture, a new era of science will begin. Now we are still in the mindset of looking at matter with a view of finding ways to manipulate and organise it for the needs of human beings. We as a society are not yet at the stage of actively trying to understand higher-level things, how the movement of energy takes place between infinity and matter, and then back again to infinity. But on the individual level, we can practise and free ourselves from everything that locks us by knowledge. We can develop our creative sense and explore. Creativity can gradually change the world. The energy form will be changing, and that will change the material form.

AM: One of the reasons I really am enjoying talking to you is that we in the West have developed philosophical, religious and social systems of a certain kind which are very powerful, but in some ways, they have reached their limits and need refreshing from an entirely different source. I have discovered in China in general and talking to you in particular that you are opening out new ways of thinking about the world which aren't present in my system of thought. This is what China is doing, I think, for the whole world at all sorts of levels, politically, socially, economically. And you are doing it in terms of aesthetics and philosophy. I feel you are guiding me towards things which I have always been interested in but have not found anyone who can explain them to me.

TY: It is my pleasure.

I have a question about science. I've always believed that scientific thinking is very important for understanding. When I talk to scientists, I feel very lucky that I'm an artist, because scientists have to keep track of many, many different considerations to be able to say, *maybe* this is like this. Scientists can never be 100% correct. There is just data and many experiments, and there are always exceptions. I am very curious to understand scientific symbolism, the way scientific notation is related to the physical world. Like Einstein's famous equation about energy.

AM: In some ways I am the wrong person to ask about science because I never did any science. It was possible in my day and age not to do any basic science – no chemistry, no physics. And mathematics only at a very humble level. So, I have never done any science, and my only knowledge of it, really, as you mentioned, is interviewing. I have interviewed about fifty scientists, ten Nobel Prize winners, one double Nobel Prize winner, and others who would win Nobel Prizes if they were in the right field: mathematicians, for example, can't get Nobel Prizes. I have talked to them, and my interest overlaps with yours, which is that I spend a lot of time on their childhood and on their early education, their interests and hobbies and what led them into that particular obsession, what generated the curiosity. Sometimes you can find that as children they were very interested in the natural world, in insects and birds, and they became biologists and so on. Some of them seemed to be born mathematicians from very early on, more or less infancy, but you don't always find that. There was one whom I interviewed, Sir John Gurdon, and at his school, Eton, his science master said, John, you are absolutely no good at science; give it up, and when you go to university study something other than science. So, he came to Cambridge and started, but he went back to science and won a Nobel Prize. He is behind much of the work in stem cell research, and there is a Gurdon Institute here in Cambridge now. He only discovered his science in his twenties, and I have met one or two people like that.

I think that one of the things I have learned from working with these people is that the gap between science and the arts is very, very thin, and that scientists don't really work in a different way

This is said by Einstein; one of his remarks is that science is only common sense. It is just ordinary thinking but concentrated and prolonged, and so he constantly says, anyone could do what I did if they had applied themselves. One of his nice quotations is, when he was asked why he had achieved what he did, he said, 'It is only because I continued to ask the questions I asked as a child, and I applied, I was very persistent, I worked hard, I concentrated.' Anyone can do that, so there is really no difference.

You were talking about getting things right, and Einstein was also aware that you don't have to get things exactly right. Another one of my favourite quotations from him is, 'It is better to get things roughly right than precisely wrong.' Get the general picture, don't spend your whole life trying to get it precisely right. Philosophers of science have pointed out that you *can't* get it absolutely right. There is no 'right': it is only better or less good, and there is always uncertainty. Even before the discovery of uncertainty and quantum theory people knew that you go as far as you can, but you can't prove anything absolutely. One experiment, as Einstein said, can *disprove* it, so you live in hope and get it as good as you can, but then someone will come along one day and show it's wrong.

Science is an art, and in many of the discussions I had with scientists they said it's about imagination, intuition. One of the contemporaries of Einstein's was the great mathematician Poincaré, who more or less came to the same conclusions about relativity. He had written a very good account of his science and one of his famous phrases is 'guessing before demonstrating'. Science doesn't work from experimental proofs, it doesn't work in the way that most people think, which is that you have a laboratory, and you do very accurate tests, and then you find something. It works by what's known technically as the hypothetico-inductive method: first a hypothesis, then induction working out from that hypothesis. The guessing comes first, sometimes guessing aided by deduction, and then comes testing of that guess and seeing if it was a good guess.

I talked to someone who had worked with Crick and Watson – they discovered the double-helix structure of the genome. He had worked with Crick a lot, and he said, we just spent our whole time guessing. They worked just over the road there. He said, we had a blackboard, so we'd just go up to it and I'd scribble some stuff on it, and Crick would say, no, that's no good, but how about this. Einstein said, 'I guess a hundred times; ninety-nine times I'm wrong, one time I'm right', so, just as an artist does – trying this out, trying that out – this is how great scientists work.

Technicians and people at a lower level may think you just look through microscopes and find things, but you've got to know they're there before you find them. This is another point that many people made: you've got to *know* the answer before you *find* the answer. You don't search vaguely for an answer, you know it's probably there and you go down to it, so science seems to me… – and it was the privilege of being at Cambridge when I met these great scientists that helped me realise this – science seems not at all different from what you do. Except in some branches of science you try and *replicate* previously obtained results in other laboratories, but even that method is a bit doubtful now, because of quantum theory: at the micro level anyway, you can do the same experiment and get different results – but not at the macro level. For instance, all the experiments they've done with Einstein's theories have shown they're still right at the macro level, but at the micro level they're not. I don't know if that's a satisfactory answer for you.

TY: Quantum mechanics looks at uncertainty, and it turns out that matter doesn't keep its form and becomes a wave. I would have liked to be a scientist because they study facts and determine what is right and wrong from that. Art has no constraints in that way. It's an emotional expression, so you can draw a circle to denote a human being. Symbolism points to a different place, and I am extremely interested in patterns. Patterns mean something. They had meaning before humans, before forms were given names. We might call some form 'dog', but the form is not the same as a name, and the pattern encompasses thousands of different dogs. Various proteins are made, organic reactions take place, which creates many, many different instances of this 'dog' form. They have different appearances, sizes, colours, depending on many factors, including the geographical conditions they live in, just as Darwin said. Every pattern contains the basic characteristics, like shape of the body, head, etc., but also a large range of less clearly defined features. Patterns appear in drawings, for example the distinctive patterns of Islamic art. Patterns point to something beyond in the ancient time. Patterns also come up in mathematics, which is a product of the human mind on the one hand, but also present in nature on the other hand, for example in crystals. Ice has a perfect structure which is very different from animals. Because I am used to drawing things, I know the different energy forms practically, the shapes that make the drawing look like a dog, or make a cat look different from a tiger. I think we have to truly combine art and science and start another way of knowing. Not strictly constrained by facts, but not completely without constraints either. Then we can really know, and then we will see physical matter in a different way.

AM: Two points on that. One is that a famous description of Darwinian evolution is 'random variation and selective retention'. The genes vary randomly, but you keep the good mutations. That's how science works, and that's why Crick and Watson did random variations. What the laboratory does is to speed that up, because if you just allow it to nature, it randomly varies, and then human beings maintain it or animals maintain it, so it takes hundreds of years. A scientific laboratory compresses time and space, and makes random variations and selective retention very-very fast, which is one of the reasons why artificial intelligence is speeding up science: it makes that testing process faster and faster, and that's why all sorts of new inventions and developments are going to occur.

The other thing you mentioned concerns symbolism. Looking at a piece of Chinese calligraphy, that's science. I mean, that's what scientists do: each of those symbols is a half-symbol, as you know.

They are logograms, they are an intersection between a symbol and a sign. In other words, they were originally pictures, and the relationship between them and reality was very close, but now they've been half-symbolised, so that when the Chinese use these half-symbols to read, they don't think of a tree or a man when they see the symbol for tree or man, they are using a slightly arbitrary symbolic way of denoting things by concentrating meaning into some characters – and so, they do exactly what scientists do. When Feynman scrawls his theories up in the symbolic notation of mathematics, he's doing what the Chinese do when they write – it's no different.

TY: I am very interested in understanding and re-understanding how things come up and how they become the way they are. I wonder how traditional cultures stayed for such a long time with a few patterns. They looked at them again and again, and they repeated them again and again in their art. There must have been some energy in these patterns that made them feel safe. It's not as simple as power in the society because women in China didn't have power, except maybe some influence within the family. In most other ways, it's a man's world. But there is a very famous handicraft, a kind of embroidery made by women, and there they created an amazing world.

AM: There was even a women's language in medieval China, a special language that only women knew and no man could understand.

TY: Because they are outside the system. Or rather, they are inside the system, but they have limited space in it. Their activities are limited, so they would gather in one room or maybe a small garden, and they would always be there, thinking about men.

AM: Well, this is another matter, but in the famous Chinese novel *A Dream of Red Mansions*[7] women are very powerful in their own worlds, the private worlds of the 'red mansion' – outside is

---

7 紅樓夢, literally 'red chamber dream'.

different.

We've got 20 minutes or so before lunch, and I wondered if we could both ask the same question: I'll ask it to you first, and then you'd can ask me the same question. It's quite a big question, and I'd be very interested to hear your comments: if you had to summarise your understanding of Chinese civilisation in five points, what would they be?

TY: Dao and Confucius. Dao encompasses a lot, and Confucius is the structure. Just these two already include many things.

AM: You can expand them out a bit. With Confucianism you've got order, harmony, hierarchy, family.

TY: The Chinese are orderly and also poetic. And image-preoccupied. For a long time, they thought that China was the whole world. That there is the sky, and the earth is China.

AM: Yes. They called China the Middle Kingdom.

TY: That's why they have problems with science and practical things, and all the artists are against the practical. During the Song dynasty, art flourished, but the empire was corrupt. As with the example of their thinking that the whole world is China, they were status-conscious but not very practical. They were too focussed on the relationship and didn't manage to get exactly what they want. Modern Chinese are the same.

How would you answer this question for the West?

AM: Well, the West is split. There are the Continental countries like France, Spain and Italy, which have certain cultural and social features which are different from what is now known as the Anglosphere, which is Britain, America and countries like that. So, if I went to the Anglosphere, it's much more extreme. Thinking about the whole West, you have to have five things. The first thing is Greek thought. Not just science and mathematics, but Greek philosophy and the way in which Greek logic works, which is different from Chinese logic. It has devices for proving theorems and exploring nature, which are absent in China. Greek thought and logic is one of the great characteristics of the West.

The second is monotheism, the belief in one God, which includes and starts with Judaism, the Jewish religion, and then spreads out into Christianity and then Islam, which creates a philosophy and culture which is totally different from Chinese Daoist polytheistic systems. So, that's the second difference. The first is philosophical, the second is religious and ritual.

The third is political, because the West is based on conquest empires, from Alexander the Great through the Romans, through the medieval civilisations. Civilisations were based on war and conquest and developed into empires. Countries rise and fall by conquering, holding and then losing. That in turn is tied to political systems, which are called feudal, where you have a ruler, but he has to have lots of people he delegates power to. They become very large landholders, they're given territories, and in return they serve the king. The Qin Emperor abolished feudalism in China. He set up a bureaucratic Mandarin intellectual system, so you have unarmed retainers, and you have a huge emphasis on education and on verbal and mental skills. So, the political systems in the two parts of the world are totally different. One is derived from feudalism and empire, and the other is derived from centralisation and a top-down hierarchy.

Another deep difference, which is difficult to explain, is that, if you bring those things together, all our philosophies are based on opposites – 'this is right, that is wrong', 'this is black, that is white', 'this is male, that is female', 'this is evil, that is good' – and these opposites are in conflict all the time. It's binary, like binary computers, whereas Chinese systems are based on yin/yang, both/and – a bit of each in the other. As you were saying earlier, ordinary matter has dark matter in it, it's not just matter. In China you combine things through harmony, whereas in the West you separate them, and the power comes out through splitting them In China and then having a clash between them. It's always a war in the West, there is always competition and war, and that leads to the last feature, an entirely different economic system.

Our economic system, from very early on, and as documented later by people like Adam Smith and others, is competitive and confrontational. Right at the beginning of the great text on this, which is *The Wealth of Nations* by Adam Smith, he says that human beings love to barter and to haggle. That means they love to try and get better outcomes from selling. Now the Chinese do this all the time, they are the great barterers. I just have to go with my Chinese friends to a shop and they are saying, oh, you know, can you do a deal on that, so the Chinese are at a petty level in day-to-day bartering – but at the higher level trade is win-win, as, for example, is shown now in the philosophy which the Chinese government is trying to promote in the world: trade benefits you and it benefits me, we are not in competition, we can work together. The West doesn't believe that; it believes that if you gain something I lose something, so we have a highly competitive game theory of economics, whereas China has a unified-and-working-together kind of philosophy.

Basically, for the last 2,000 years all the premises of the West and the Chinese have been entirely different, and our job in talking to each other is to try and map them onto each other.

TY: China thinks in terms of family and hierarchy, and the West tries to build systems. When the West is in control of some place, they impose their rules and systems. A Chinese emperor might conquer another country, and then he would create a certain situation where if that country doesn't go against China, they can live as they want. China is preoccupied with status. The West is based on class, I think. Western systems protect the higher classes. If you aren't of a certain class, you can't go through certain doors.

AM: Exclusive.

TY: Yes. In the case of China, if you are part of the extended family, you live under the big umbrella and protection of China. Even when there were scientific advances in China, and things like gunpowder were invented, China felt no need to develop such inventions to conquer more and more, or to constantly think about protecting itself. In order to think this way, you have to have the mentality of always fighting outside and subjecting other peoples to your systems. But with China, as long as the relationship within the family was good and the empire orderly, the emperor felt safe and content. That's the difference between China and the West. When the West became powerful, it didn't understand this about China.

AM: This is an important point in international relations. I think China is like the galaxy where you have the Middle Kingdom, the Sun – and then the family. That's the metaphor they use. Vietnam, Burma, Korea, Japan are the younger brothers. China is the older brother or the father, and so we behave as we do to the family. The family will not benefit if I kill my younger brother, but my younger brother must show some respect for me, and in return I will show some respect and help him. That metaphor of familistic international relations is totally different from what happens in the West. In the West you are the central dominant force, and those others are your enemies, and the only way you can keep them in control is to exert power over them, economic and social power to keep them in check, otherwise they will rise up against you.

We've got time perhaps for one last question each, which is similar to the previous one but about something else: if you had to summarise your understanding of traditional Chinese aesthetics in five points, what would they be?

TY: In Chinese we have *xing shen ge yi* (形神格意). *Xing* is 'form'. *Shen* is 'spirit'. When I see this word, I feel myself on another – nonphysical – level. *Ge*[8] is something unexplainable because this

8 An elusive notion, something like 'style' or 'taste'.

notion belongs on a high level that is not open to ordinary people. *Ge* can be known only by those who have risen high in their level of perception. *Yi* is 'imagination', the higher poetic. It has to be broken and become imperfect because when you are not perfect, you jump to an even higher level. This is why the Chinese always talk about breaking what's perfect and reaching infinity. All substance is primitive; you have to break it and become infinity, become real art. This is why we say that things are not real, but they have a special feeling. The saying *xu shi bing zhi* (虚实并置) means that, for example, when I am talking about this cup, it exists and at the same time does not exist. In the physical world the cup takes up some space, but when we try to describe the entire space, it's another thing. The cup cuts out some space. It's like shadow space, and this is why we talk about existing and not existing at the same time. It's the difference between seeing things in time and outside of time, like a mirroring effect. The same applies to me: I am here, and I am not here at the same time. Positive energy and negative energy coexist as a balance of infinite force at the same time. It's difficult to explain, to put into words. I call it *xuan xu* (玄虚), unfathomable.

AM: It gets easier once you start thinking in yin/yang quantum way: in quantum theory the cat exists and doesn't exist at the same time. We are now getting used to the idea of things being their opposite at the same time, but even 50 years ago people would have found it difficult to deal with such an idea.

TY: Yes, this isn't easy to understand. Now is a good time for conversations of this kind. For example, Lili also exists and doesn't exist at the same time. The appearance of a girl is here, she does take up space, but at the same time she does not exist. I would say that it's one thing to be within time and another to be outside time. This is what the ancient Chinese are talking about: when you are outside time, everything is there all at once, and when you are inside the time, you will be seeing all the ordinary things surrounding you. Sometimes you have to get outside of time and see the translucence of reality. Sometimes Lili replaces me in a way. She is replacing my existence when I'm taking pictures and becomes my world and becomes my language. I don't even do anything because she is there, and suddenly, oh, the world is not on, and we are going to see something in between being and non-being. This 'in between' is very powerful because, as you said, matter is just five percent of the world, and we are living in the understanding of those five percent. In order for matter to exist in front of us as physical objects, there has to be big power surrounding these objects because energy concentrates and gives rise to matter. It is a huge amount of energy.

AM: Does it relate to chi at all? You often talk about energy, and Westerners now are beginning to know about Tai Chi and the power of chi as energy. Is that partly what you are referring to?

TY: Yes. Chi is not a thing. It is something invisible. Like wind, for example, it is a force, something that makes things move. Chi is more complicated because it's energy, so a person of high energy perceives the world differently, in a more clear and intense way. It is not just physical.

AM: Just two last questions related to that. As a Westerner and a non-artist, my thought about Chinese art is that if you want to understand it, you have to realise that it is all about symbols. Nothing exists in itself, everything exists in relation to something else, everything is pointing out from itself to something else – every character, every colour. We in the West tend to objectify things, and we say, this is red – but the Chinese look at red and say, this is female, this is autumn… both in language and in art everything is standing for many-many different things. For example, when you read modern poetry by Xu Zhimo in Chinese, you don't just read the words like we do in English. Every word he uses is pointing to some Tang poet or some experience of someone else. Is that correct?

TY: You know, in old Chinese literature there is *fu bi xing* (賦比興)[9]. The middle sign is *bi*, which means 'to refer'. For example, when I am sad, I would talk about trees and how their leaves are falling. The feeling inside of the last leaf falling – it's talking about something on another level, reflected through another thing. The Chinese talk about *xing er shang shi xue* (形而上诗学). It is the poetic way of seeing the physical world on another level, being the world through your heart and your senses. I think this is talking about energies, not about the practical world, but it is also something reflected in the physical world. It's about looking at something that exists both physically and on a higher level. We call it *fei sheng* (飛升), which means levitating. This way of being above the ground keeps one's morals and mind clear, seeing the diversity of things, but at the same time not being grounded by anything. It's like a cloud. The ground is the physical activities, the mundane aspects of life. The cloud is untouched by these. It is a way for us to always be away from ourselves, just as Bruce Lee talked about emptying yourself.

AM: That's a good Buddhist thought.

One more question about understanding Chinese art. We in the West live in the post-Renaissance period, where we have separated the eye and the ear, whereas in Chinese writing, certainly, you read it with your eyes and you read it with your ear at the same time, so there has been no separation. A Chinese painting is not just a painting, as it is in the West, it is not realist or surrealist or anything else, it is depiction and language at the same time, because it is almost calligraphy carried to a further extent, so when you see the traditional Chinese paintings with mountains, rivers, flowers and so on, it is a form of calligraphy at the same time as being a painting. They haven't separated out, and so Chinese art has double power, because it appeals through the eyes and through the ears. Is that roughly right?

TY: In ancient times, the most excellent artists were almost like

---

9 A principle of organising the poem in a three-fold way: *fu* is a narrative detailing a certain situation; *bi* (lit. 'against') is a contrast achieved by placing two things or situations side by side; from contemplating *bi*, the reader experiences *xing*, a flash of insight into *fu*. Confucius was of the opinion that *xing* is the purpose of poetry.

hermits. They attained a high spiritual level and didn't socialise with others. They drank a lot and spent their time alone in the higher reality and their art. Earlier I talked about the cloud. Everyone is looking for that connection, but the cloud doesn't give any definitions or explanations; you have to feel it. When you see good calligraphy, it exudes a certain power that isn't physical but from another reality. Good art energises the person looking at it, and the original purpose of exhibiting art was transmission of energy. When I feel weak, I look at old art, and it raises me to another level. When you are looking at art, you get into it, and you have to feel satisfaction doing it. With bad art, you go in, and there is nothing. But good art you can look at for a long time because it continues transferring energy to you. High-level artists didn't engage in long planning of their works. They would start a painting almost accidentally and go with the momentum, and you'd see how it all came together only after they finished it.

AM: Well, that explains it... One of the most famous Chinese Tang poets drowned while trying to touch the moon's reflection in the river after drinking a great deal.

TY: Li Bai?

AM: Yes. Your comment that alcohol was an important part of poetry reminds us that we should go and have a drink or a meal...

*

AM: What influence has Buddhism had on your art?

TY: I think I was influenced by Buddhism from a young age, through my teachers. They talked about silence and movement, about yin-yang and other basic things. When I was a teenager, I was really influenced by Western art, like Impressionism, Post-Impressionism and Surrealism. At that time my teacher was a painter, and he had a lot of students. He was painting Western paintings in abstract style. He built up the rhythm and the contrast, and his style was sort of realistic but in abstract form.

So, for instance, a building looked like a building but was rendered abstractly. I learned a lot from him, I think. I modified and used what I had learned from him in my photography, painting and movies. I used his teachings a lot and later found out that much of it came from Buddhism. I wasn't familiar with Dao at that time. But after some time, I realised that what I thought of as Buddhism was mostly Dao. When Buddhism came to China, it changed and combined with Dao. So, Buddhism in China is different from Buddhism in India. Buddhism influenced Zen a lot. Zen is close to Dao, but it came from Buddhism under Japanese influence. We in China don't know much about the original Buddhism from India, except from the outside. But with Dao we know that there is no structure for understanding everything. There are many things. These things have their own rhythm. They are all individual and formed by chance. The diversity and the many layers of things are contemplated all at once. It is *guan gu jin yu xu yu, fu si hai yu yi shun* (观古今于须臾，抚四海于一瞬), which means 'observe the past and present in an instant, embrace the world in a moment'. Everything is together, and everything is contemplated together. This gave me a strong sense of calm and taught me to observe calmly. It's another way to channel the passion to fulfil what I want to do. So, maybe you could say that Buddhism influenced me in this way, though from my Indian friends I got an impression that Buddhism there is different. It seems to emphasise continuity. In Zen, every moment everything disappears and then *pop!* – it reappears. It is empty, but it is there. Dao is about continuity, looking for the path. It is not just one point, but the movement. It is different from the Japanese. The Japanese focus on the moment. In China, the focus is on the path. In the Chinese garden, you are not expected to stand still and look at it. It is not like the Western garden either, where there is structure. In the Chinese garden, you walk. In the Stone Forest, there is water underneath, so you walk and listen to the sound of water. Everything is about the path. The path to another way and the mirroring to another place. These teachings are part of my life. I look at things in this way.

AM: One influence Zen had, in Japan anyway, was to simplify things, to make everything as simple and clear as possible. And to purify things, so that the colours in Zen art are black and white. Very simple colours, not extremes. And the forms are as simple as possible. Is that part of an influence on you or not?

TY: I think Zen influenced all of us because it's so simple and so powerful. Like Akira Kurosawa, the filmmaker. He talks about human relationships, human difficulties, big themes in human lives. I think Kurosawa is transforming Western knowledge into a traditional form.

AM: Yes, Kurosawa is a very good example.

TY: Yes, he's the West and East combined.

AM: Especially when he does Shakespeare – like *Ran*.

The next question is, what is your understanding of freedom?

TY: That's a very good question. For me freedom is a feeling of harmony. For example, if I sit here and feel comfortable, I feel I can think about what I want to think about and do what I want to do. I feel free to do it, and I feel respected. I feel that what I do is welcomed and others are happy for me to do it. Freedom is about relationships. People might feel defensive or worried about something or someone, but when you have good energy together, they feel comfortable, relaxed, and everyone can speak freely. Freedom is not an individual thing. I think people who think just about individual freedom are really dangerous.

AM: You think it's really dangerous?

TY: Yes. If I feel free in an individual way, I may want to sit in this chair. Nobody else can sit in it because when I sit there, nobody else can. The real freedom is that I don't sit in the chair and give freedom to other people to sit in it. So, everyone can sit in the chair and there is no conflict. But when I'm sitting in the chair, there will be conflict: nobody can sit in it because I'm here.

This was a deep realisation when I did the first *Love Infinity*. Everyone was talking about self-expression, about property, about class, and this makes things difficult. Everyone is going to feel uncomfortable. Higher classes would be worried about change. Lower classes would feel passed over. The rich would worry that other people might be richer than them. But when everyone doesn't want to sit in the chair, everyone is free.

AM: One of the big differences between China and the West is in relation to the concept of individual rights and freedom. I have the right: property rights, or place rights, or class rights, or the right to carry guns, or whatever the rights are. And some people think that the West tries to impose an extreme emphasis on individual rights on other countries: you have the right to elect, you as a woman have equal rights with men and so on.

TY: I think some of these things are just attempts to restore harmony. Women were mistreated for a long time, and now we are trying to create balance between women and men. Ordinary people were bullied by rich and powerful people in the past, so now we are trying to give rights to ordinary people to restore the balance.

AM: Right. Your turn now for a question.

TY: Up till now, you have travelled to the east, and you have travelled to the west. What is 'the west' and what is 'the east' for you today?

AM: Well, when I was in Japan and asked my friends, where is the West, they said, oh, China. It is not just that China is socially (family etc.), politically and historically so different, but that its mix of Confucianism, Daoism and Buddhism feels very different to Japan, as does its art and even language. And when I asked people in China where is the West, they said, oh, obviously India. That's the West. When I ask people in in India, they say Israel and Saudi Arabia are the West. The monotheisms, political and social systems of the Middle East feel very different to many

Indians. In other words, anything to their west is their notion of 'the West'.

When *we* think about 'the West', we think about ourselves and America. So basically, it's all relative. Looking from here, we talk about degrees of eastness. We consider ourselves the West. The Middle East then is Palestine, Saudi Arabia, and so on. I think for us 'the East' begins at China and India.

Although it's more difficult than that. There's a very well-known book by Edward Said called *Orientalism*. 'The Orient' means 'the east'. But curiously, his book starts at the Middle East – that's the Orient for Said – and it stops there. There's nothing about India, nothing about China, nothing about Japan: the Orient for Said is what we call the Middle East.

Perhaps the other thing to say is that the boundaries keep shifting. I think, if you'd asked me that question early in my life, I would have said, well, India, China, those sorts of places are the East, and we are the West. Now, I often think more about the colours of the rainbow, so that you get a sort of gradual transition from one colour into the next colour. For me, the extreme West is my own culture in England and America. But already when I'm in southern Europe, which has been quite strongly influenced by the East, particularly by the conquests of Islam, I sense the East much more there. If you go to southern Spain, and even Venice, and parts of the Mediterranean area, you get these shapes and smells and feelings of the traders who came in over the centuries into the Mediterranean. There is a touch of the East the moment you get over the Channel, but certainly when you get down to southern France, Italy and so on. So, the East begins a little bit there, and then the Middle East, which I hardly know, is probably 'the East' a little bit more, but not much more because it's Islamic.

It really starts in India; the smells, the philosophies, the religions, the absence of monotheism starts in India. But I can see why the Chinese and Japanese think that India is 'the West', because there is a huge invisible barrier on which there are one or two countries like Burma and Thailand. Once you get through them and certainly beyond India, you get into something which is very, very different. As you say, the form of Buddhism is very different, the form of art is different, the food is different, philosophies are different. And so, there are different easts, just as there are different wests. It's a bit of a confused answer, but eastness and westness shift.

I remember that a Head of my College, an anthropologist, was asked to set up a new discussion group called 'The south-east Asia'. And he rather upset the people who were setting it up by coming to the launch and saying, there is no such thing: south of what? east of what? It has no meaning. So, 'south-east Asia' doesn't really have much meaning.

Then again, even within China, if you are from Guangdong or Fujian, you might well say that 'the West' begins in Sichuan and Yunnan. Yunnan and Xinjiang, they've got quite a lot of influence from the West along the Silk Roads. So, the West begins in Xinjiang. And then at the other extreme, Shanghai is very Western. And Hong Kong, obviously. So, that's my answer to that one.

TY: In early times, when China was governed by Mongolians, and Marco Polo arrived and saw this amazing land, how do you think this influenced the West to try to understand the East? Was it through imagination or another way? Later the West developed the image of 'Oriental dreams'. There was also increased interest in India, and in mid-Renaissance times Chinese ceramics became very trendy.

AM: The more we know about archaeology and history, the more we can see that the two ends of Eurasia are connected. You can see influences from Roman and Greek art in early Chinese heads in the buried terracotta army faces, and some of the statues, and very early Qin art.

The influence also goes the other way round, for example in

Chinese musical instruments. I was talking to a great expert on Chinese music, and he said a lot of influences come through the Silk Road from Egypt. Some of the language that you can find in some of the minority written scripts is the same as Egyptian. We know more and more about the way these ideas flow, not necessarily with people but traders who pass them to the next person and so on.

I think even before Marco Polo there were earlier travellers, and the West knew certain things about China already. In the 8th-9th century, during the Tang, along the east coast of China there were Jewish people coming into the cities, in Fujian and elsewhere; there were Western churches; there was a mosque in one of the cities, Xiamen. Xiamen's got a lot of Western influence from the 8th-9th century. Five hundred years before Marco Polo there were traders coming from the West to China. And so, there were big influences.

One or two of the strange things, though, are that the four great inventions of China – gunpowder, compass, printing press and silk – took a long time to come to the West. Of course, that's partly the Chinese trying to protect the secrets of silk, but gunpowder doesn't really come into the West until the 11th-12th century, the printing press quite a bit later, and the compass roughly the same time. So, it took some hundreds of years in a number of cases for these macro-inventions to travel across, and yet I think at the micro-level of style, art, philosophy and so on the transmission was quicker.

The last thing to say is about Marco Polo. We have a friend, Frances Wood, who wrote a book called *Did Marco Polo Go to China?* She's a member of our group and she was the curator of the Dunhuang collections in the British Museum. She argued very strongly that there is no evidence and indeed there is some negative evidence: there are things that he misses – for example, he doesn't mention tea; surely, anyone who was writing about China would mention tea. On the other hand, and I've discussed this with her, there are things in Marco Polo's account which you couldn't have known except if someone had been to China. It might not have been him, and anyway Marco Polo was probably several people put together, but they recently dug up a boat – again, somewhere like Xiamen – and they found it contained a brilliant Chinese invention which is airlocks. In other words, you make the boat with little bits where you keep air in separate compartments, so if a rock hits the boat it doesn't sink. That's an early Chinese invention, and Marco Polo mentions that in his account. He couldn't have known that, or it couldn't have been known unless someone had brought that knowledge from China. Now you could say, well, some earlier Arab traders might have looked at the boats and noticed that the Chinese had this wonderful idea – so it doesn't prove it either way. But reading Marco Polo's account of Suzhou, for example, and comparing it to the scrolls – the famous scrolls of paintings of going up the river in the Spring Festival – his account is so similar that I find it a little difficult to think that *someone* didn't go to China at about that time. That's my guess.

TY: A lot of mystery there. There are stories about his father being a merchant and sailing long distances.

AM: Of course, you know the story very well. You were involved in making the series of films on Marco Polo on Netflix, and it was so violent, so much killing, that I was only allowed to watch one episode before my wife stopped me, saying, I can't watch any more of this, there's too much killing. But in that first episode was the story of how the father said to the Emperor, you can keep my son, and I'm off.

TY: I think many things were made up. I know the script writer, John Fusco. He's a big fan of Chinese culture.

AM: Fantasy. It did say, I think, at the beginning of the film that, although some of the events were real, some of them were also invented. That was probably another reason my wife wouldn't watch it.

Let me ask another question. This is about Lili. You said, I think, in our first discussion or elsewhere, that Lili is fake. What is real? What is the opposite of fake?

TY: For me, the real should come from an original form. Artificial intelligence is just recording reactions of living people. I am real because I am continuous, related to an earlier state of me. Artificial intelligence performs calculations with numbers, and based on these calculations it has a number of options of how to act. The behaviour of a real thing is softer, more nuanced. That's because the machine can only process a certain number of data points to determine its behaviour, and anything in excess of that number is beyond the machine's capacity. It is just like any other medium we have. Even a very high-quality photograph is different from the real. The real is more.

AM: Is a photograph real or fake?

TY: This is a very interesting question. Is an image real or fake? It is changing every moment. We think we are living in the same continuously changing physical world. But is that real? Are we able to keep track of everything in this world? There are very many aspects, all of them changing all the time, but our eyes can't keep track of all this at once. If something doesn't change sufficiently continuously, we can't keep track of that thing. Such things eventually fade from our attention. Many, many things are happening to which we are oblivious, and there is a good reason to ask what is real. In talking about what is real we talk about a point of view. Also, time and space are needed for deciding if something is real. This cup is real because it is in this time and space. Without time and space, we cannot say what is real and what isn't, what exists and what doesn't. We can talk about possibilities. In fact, I've always believed that we are living in a possibility. To me that is the real thing. Many layers of possibility. We try hard to understand how one instant is related to another. Human beings have always thought about this.

AM: As you know, this is discussed by a lot of philosophers, for example David Hume. Since it's a whole set of discrete moments, I am what I am now, but in an hour's time, am I the same person as I am now? Time has passed, and things have changed in the body, so is it the same person or a different person?

TY: That is tricky too. If we take 100 people, they all have different perspectives from which they view the world, and different levels of perception. But when we talk about things, language creates the illusion of a single perspective. It creates a limitation. If I say that something is big, then whoever has a perspective similar to mine would agree with me. But a giant probably wouldn't. When we are using language, we need to be careful about who we are talking to and who is talking. So, when I receive a question, I always ask where the question came from. Depending on that, the same question can have different answers. Poetic language helps us escape from certain limitations of language. Its perspective is less physical. Spiritual level affects perspective and perception. People on a higher spiritual level communicate differently from those whose perception is more limited. They communicate from a higher and wider vantage point. So, when we talk about what is real, we should first find out who is asking the question and who is answering it. Is God answering the question? Is one of the people asking the question? What is real depends on the level of perception of time and space. People whose perception of time and space is similar would have a similar range of things they consider real.

AM: In Zen there is no distinction between fake and real. There is no real 'real' and there is no fake because the inner essence is empty anyway.

TY: I have talked to Zen people quite a bit, including my brother who is a Zen monk. I always have questions for them. The Japanese garden is very different from the Chinese garden. The Japanese garden is still. Everything is still, and out of the stillness arises a constantly moving universe. You are sitting at a distance from all the movement, and you have to empty yourself to perceive the truth about movement and outward appearances.

The Chinese garden is not like that. You have to walk, look at things, take in smells. There is something called *ying bi* (影壁)[10]. It is the empty frame. The empty frame is recording the surrounding shadows, and the rain. So, they feel like they are in a passage. The Chinese also talk about *dang xia* (当下), which means 'that moment'. Everything is about that moment. One instant there is substance. Then it disappears, and there is nothing. In another instant the substance reappears. There is just this appearing and disappearing of substance. A previous appearance of substance seems to affect the next appearance of substance, which we see as movement. Something invisible is making substance reappear from emptiness again and again. But at the same time, it is empty. Zen talks about that grey area, between substance and emptiness. They say everything is nothing. They focus on the invisible spiritual world. One has to concentrate intensely to perceive it. One has to study to attain that level of concentration. They don't want to use language to talk about this because using language brings in limitations. The movement is stillness. It is silence. But the Chinese don't talk about the silence. They talk about the movement, about perceiving the whole space and how everything is together at once. And disappears at once. It is much bigger, I think.

AM: Fascinating.

TY: I would love to ask a personal question. From your books I understood that you have a very interesting family. You travelled a lot. You live in a house with a beautiful garden and land. There are many things that influenced you, not just your education. You have a certain relationship with nature, with space. Then you started to go to the East. There must be something that made you want to learn more about the differences between the West and the East. Maybe you feel something in nature. You received an excellent education, and it taught you intellectual understanding and knowledge of conceptual systems. But now you want to go in a different direction. Because you have accumulated enough

10 Hidden space.

systematic background and intellectual understanding already, and you are looking for the next stage.

When I was shooting *Love Infinity* and talking to young people and the artists, they seem to talk more and more about the spiritual. In the 20th century there were major developments in physical science, and the scientific way of thinking reached a very high level. But now it's become excessive, and maybe there is need to balance it. I don't know. But I can see that people are starting to look for ways of balancing.

How do you feel about this? It seems that you went through these stages in your life. The scientific, intellectual stage, and then your later interests.

AM: There are two questions I took out of that.

The first one is, having gone through a very standard but high-quality Western education which seemed to have educated me to a level where I had the tools to understand my world (as a historian, anyway), why did I then go into a new discipline, anthropology, and why did I go to other parts of the world than England? As with all things one does, there are many different factors: my mother's interest in India and the Far East, and the fact she wanted me to go back to that part of the world, and the fact I was born there. But you can impose a pattern on your past which probably didn't exist at the time.

What I like to think is that I discovered the limits of the world I was brought up in. I could see that it could answer some questions quite well, but I was living inside what Wittgenstein the philosopher calls a 'fly-bottle'. That is, a bottle in which you keep a fly. We can't escape from the fly-bottle but we can know that it is there, we can know where the glass is, and he said that our aim in philosophy is to try and do that. Instead of just hitting it here and there you say, ah yes, I'm in a fly-bottle, this is the limit. He defined philosophy, to a certain extent, as finding out the limits of what you can know and what language can do. And so, I like to think that I was brought up, to a certain extent, in a disappointing education because I sensed there were things missing in it.

There was also a sense of loss: throughout my childhood and adolescence I was aware that I was losing as much as I was gaining. It's the feeling that you get in one of our great poets, Wordsworth, that there were things you knew when you were a child: you seemed to be connected to nature and landscape, things had meaning, God was there, and spirit, and so on. What people often call enchantment, an enchanted landscape. I had the sense that in my childhood I was within enchantment but through my education and adolescence it was fading away. It's the central theme of our greatest period of poetry which is the Romantic movement. If you look at Keats, Shelley, Wordsworth, Coleridge and Blake, it's all about the loss of that enchantment, of connectedness – and the movement into what Max Weber calls the 'iron cage' of rationality.

So, I clung onto the enchantment. I used to read children's stories even at university and tried to partially remain in that world, but, as it did with Wordsworth, it faded into the light of common day, which is what he describes. I wasn't going to find it in England – and it perhaps wasn't what I was consciously seeking – but certainly when I went to Nepal, to a civilisation which was enchanted, filled with spirit and meaning, and in which there was no separation, I discovered it there. The people seemed to have a meaningful life even though they were poor. They were happy. They felt whole and integrated with their world and with themselves. When I came back to England, looked at people's faces and the way they behaved, they seemed to have lost that.

Having experienced that in Nepal, when I went to Japan I found the same thing – and particularly when I went to China. In terms of pop psychology, the rational left hemisphere had taken over most of my life in my education, and it needed to be rebalanced with the imaginative right hemisphere, the heart side. I've often shown to people that on my hands the head and the heart line is the same, so it's a balance, complete balance between head and heart. My later life going to these other places was restoring the heart and the imagination, not losing what I learned before but putting the two together, and so anthropology was really an attempt to balance.

Of course, I may be projecting what I would like to happen, but in terms of what's happening now, I notice that many young people I meet are not in a hurry to learn to drive, they've turned off Facebook, and they spend a lot of time on painting, walking or travelling. They seem to have gone through the great phase of consumer affluence and mechanisation, and now they're searching and seeking for deeper spiritual things. You can even see it in very small things. For example, my village in the Fens has a magazine, and in it there are advertisements for things you can do. In the old days it would say, learn French or Spanish, but now almost every village has Tai Chi. Many of my friends use Chinese medicine and many of them are interested in philosophies of other parts of the world, so they are searching for things outside the Western tradition.

In a way it's rather nice as a move back because China and Japan became highly Westernised as they industrialised and changed, and now we are becoming more Chinese. People don't put it like that, but I think there is a search for meaning even in America, where the belief in spirits and gods and God is very high. Polls show that many people in America believe that dead people come back to life, that there are ghosts, there are spirits, so I think even in the most rational Western highly scientific societies there is search for enchantment.

And the last thing I'll say is, I wrote a book called *Enchantment and Modernity* which is about this theme, and at the end I found that most of us, most of the time are living in enchantment. We think of ourselves as rational, but most of our life is in conversation, love, music, art, games – it's enchanted – so we should stop thinking of ourselves as purely rational civilised Western people. We are as enchanted as everyone else, but in a different way.

Let me ask you one more question and then we'll finish. How can we know about the world and the inner side of things?

TY: For the East, my answer is to look more carefully at facts and learn to be more scientific. We are bombarded by news that is shaped by big companies and international committees. They are imposing on people scientific views of how the world is and what is happening in it. We are made to think that the most reliable information must come from the reports of scientists. We might act as if we have understood these things ourselves, but that's not true – these are views imposed by those in positions of influence and authority.

I think the Chinese make a mistake by always dreaming, always being imaginative. It seems that they are not taken seriously, and they feel this is normal. I think the new generation should learn how to be scientific but to retain imagination at the same time. Imagination gives you an open outlook, a curiosity to understand more, to create friendships with other people and to constantly generate fresh new energy to see deeply and widely. In my last book I kept asking, what is going on, what is going on. Noticing the undercurrents beneath outward appearances makes it possible to discern interesting things that are still in their gestational stages.

Look how the digital world started. In World War II, or even earlier, in Turing's works. The war gave this idea a strong impetus to develop. The first computers were huge machines, but technologies developed fast, and soon the digital changed the way of communications and delivering information. Look at phones, for example. Remember the payphones in the street, remember the first mobile phones, how big and heavy they were. Then phones became smaller and smaller, the Internet grew, and with the innovation of companies like Apple the development was like an explosion, growing very fast, with almost immediate feedback.

Now artificial intelligence is gathering more and more momentum. Five years ago, we wouldn't have believed that what we are seeing today was possible. The public just sees a small part of it and doesn't understand the full implications of this development. People should be ready for a big shock when these implications surface fully. Ordinary people have more to worry about. Their jobs can often be reduced to a function, AI would take over such jobs, and people would start losing their identity and feeling out of place in the society that would have different job requirements. There are also deep concerns about how society would take care of its old and weak. AI developments are not necessarily helpful to ordinary people. Every day they are getting much more information than they need. People are drowning in the sea of explosions of all this information exchange, most of which is commercially motivated, to make the machine run faster and faster.

I think it's time to balance. To balance and get everything together again.

AM: That's a nice note to end on. Thank you very much.

TY: Thank you.

Time in the Future - Robot Lili ©Tim Yip Studio

Five. 18 May 2023.

Lili – Hong Kong, Taiwan Province, Mainland China – Architecture – Living Dao – Questions from within and searching – Just find the next step – The gift of creating the normal.

AM: It's lovely to see you again. I really look forward to these sessions and I've learned so much from you. We've got some more questions. I want to start with Lili, who is sitting beside me. I can't actually ask her any questions, but I can ask you on her behalf.

TY: I can translate.

AM: Just to finish the circle, these are questions from my granddaughter Lily. I sent her some of your films, and as an artist she loved them. She asked me to ask you three questions about Lili. The first is, do you see Lili as some kind of extension of yourself, as yin to your yang, or is she a complete separate entity in herself?

TY: Lili is always bringing new questions. It's something to do with her being abstract. 'Abstract' can mean 'very simple', for example a single brush stroke is an abstract painting. But I feel abstract is something that you can't explain but it's very familiar. Before I made Lili, I wanted to make a work that is totally abstract, so I copied myself and made another human being, and let her project and reflect everything that I wanted to understand and research. That's the beginning. I think she's a kind of extension, but she's not a mere appendage.

Her being there is important in two ways. I can extend to different dimensions of seeing the work I'm making and then come back to a specific art discipline, which could be sculpture, movie, photograph or installation, so that I can pull the impressions together to reflect the things I want to, even though they are abstract and belong to all kinds of dimensions I want to invoke. I had already been doing this a lot, and because our subconscious is very difficult to read with the conscious mind, you have to be *unthinking* and then let things happen. Lili has no definitions, no aggression. She is completely reactive, and she reflects very fast. Later I found all this work was coming out. It's something like there is some kind of attitude, some kind of movement coming from her. It was affecting me because I was looking, reflecting and doing creative work, and then afterwards there was more and more of this. Sometimes I sense in her my own projection, sometimes it's someone else's. But at the same time, it seems like when she's in the photo, I can escape from this reality because she replaces me.

AM: Interesting. And her second question, which may overlap: is Lili more of an interactive art piece or an artistic collaborator? Does she work with you?

TY: For me or for what she's projecting?

AM: What she's projecting.

TY: Maybe we can have a photo with you and her, so that you can ask her yourself? She's not something fixed. When she sits with you, I will find all information from you and establish who she is, and afterward we'll take her pictures, so that suddenly you'll have an extension of what I'm feeling about you. And also, people sometimes have ideas, sometimes they have reactions, sometimes they have a really small kind of feeling that I can catch in my photographs. With Lili I know more and more about how humans coexist with other humans and also how different people see things differently.

When I am doing art direction in a movie, I work with actors who are rich and beautiful people, and I have to turn them into whatever the character is. An ordinary person, maybe with hates, fears and worries. I work to make the director and the actor understand such things. I create the whole atmosphere before the actors utter a single word, so they begin speaking and acting after the whole situation around them has been prepared by me. I take photographs and gauge what effect this or that detail would have on the reaction of the audience. In movies, apart from static setup, there is also the movement of the camera to consider, so the camera can draw attention to details by focussing on them. Every time you show something on the screen, it becomes big. A big message. The proportions are lost because proportions come from the relation, there have to be at least two things for proportions to be visible. When the camera is focussed on one object, there are no proportions, and no matter how small or big the object is, they look the same. But I am always looking for the rhythm.

I find Lili interesting because before I made her, I didn't know everything I know now, after working with her. You see, nowadays with artificial intelligence, everyone wants things to look real. They are making 3D models and making real-looking things. I didn't feel that was satisfying. It's not poetic. But Lili is like an old-fashioned puppet. Her face is not changing, but in the hands of a master puppeteer she can make you reach a surprising depth of emotion. Beijing opera has this ability too: a mere sketch can take you into the form of beauty and go deeply into your heart. When we go somewhere, I always try to pose Lili, to show how she's breathing, how she's relaxing, how she feels in this space, where is she looking, what interests her. I can pose her in different ways, using just one or two simple choices, so it's not as complicated as a real human. But she can bring up something really, really powerful. And you can feel her mirroring you. So, I think I'll keep her for a while until I find a way of going even deeper.

Now I'm trying to make her become reflective to an abstract space. Like I'm doing a quantum mechanics Lili, an alien Lili, an artificial intelligence Lili. And I'm also doing a nature Lili.

AM: So, you're making new versions of Lili?

TY: Yes. It seems like she becomes infinity mirroring what we are and how we are. She is an artwork for me to explore what is human and what is in my own mind at the subconscious level. I might feel something very difficult to put into words, but I can sense it from her. And another interesting thing is, it seems like she's opening the door of other people. People surround Lili, and I can sense their emotions and reactions from her. We can put much more detail in artworks like Lili, so that we can go further and further, even to different dimensions.

I believe in direct sensing. It's very important now in art. There is too much verbal dialogue between artists, too many concepts. But I think concepts belong to criticism, to social sciences, maybe to theory of art. I just believe in experience. My work is all about experience. When you see my work, you have to question, you have to hesitate. It's not definite. I cannot give definitions. I just want to bring in more hesitation. Hesitation makes you grow. It makes you understand more. It makes you more capable than anyone dependent on definitions. With definitions, you can't have more because it's already there. The thing is defined – what do you want to ask? Without definition you can get deeper and deeper. We're facing multiple layers of looking at things now. It's a different generation. How do we find the language of multiple sensing? You can sense me, you can sense her, you can sense everyone in the room. But the language we have now can cover just one angle. There is no one answer. We have to change the question.

Lili is endlessly evolving, pushing you or welcoming you to find more angles in things. There are so many layers every instant, and energies are focussing into one point. That's how time and space were formed, through the focussing of high energies into points. This time and space is only one form of existence. If we can come out of this time and space and look at the whole thing, there will be a somewhat similar different world, another kind of understanding. When you see that, you realise that everything is flowing like a river.

Like I said, architecture for me is like someone who has come to a strange place. When they come here, everything is uncomfortable and different from where they came from. So they tried to rebuild from earthly materials their native world, to find the memory of it. When I see the architectures of human history, it's like going back to mathematics, to geometry. Maybe this is where we came from. Geometry is a certain energy flow, it has a rhythm, a structure. I think the big difference between animals and humans is that humans can form things. Trees and other things are from nature, but humans form things that have a different origin. The shapes humans create are not from nature. But humans reflect nature and make geometry. There are many energies going out from us to nature, and we have to find balance with nature, so we stop feeling fear. We can find a new way of looking at nature's rhythm and our own rhythm. This has been put under the name 'spiritual', but I think the spiritual has been made too complicated. It's very simple. Once we find the simplicity, we'll find the harmonies of balance.

AM: Thank you, Lili. I've learned a lot from that. Tim, your turn to ask questions.

TY: We are living in a digital world, and I think we can't escape from digitisation. Maybe this is a good thing because previously we were studying continuous things, like narratives or the flow of history, and our brain couldn't deal with so much data at once. But now, thanks to digitisation, we have a smaller and therefore more manageable sampling of data, and so it's possible that very talented people might be able to cross over many disciplines. I know that you've developed databases in order to discover and study tendencies of the populations you've worked on. The database might have given you a view of all the differences and details and maybe a higher vantage point. I think the whole economy of human knowledge will be changed in about 10 or so years. Maybe it's changing already, we just can't see it yet. What do you think about all this?

AM: 'Digital' has several different meanings. One is the meaning one associates with computers and particularly with binary computers. That kind of computing is fading away, and it's being replaced by quantum. Therefore, I am not certain, I haven't talked about it, whether you can really talk about digital in relation to quantum worlds. Because they are not digital. They don't switch back and forth. So, we move beyond digital to quantum.

But in relation to my own path with digitisation, I'll just explain a little bit. When I first came to Cambridge in 1971, the computer was developing very, very fast at that time. At the time, I didn't know the full scale of what was going on, but just yesterday I discovered that not only were they inventing new forms of computer search systems just down the road from here, in the cafe, but the cognitive psychologist/computer scientist who first thought of a new kind of artificial intelligence, neural networks, was a student here in King's. Turing, who was also at King's, had thought of the general principle of artificial intelligence many years ago. Prior to Geoffrey Hinton's work, artificial intelligence worked by accumulating large amounts of information and then trying to find patterns in it, but Hinton used his psychology to design computer systems that think like human beings. He co-invented the concept of neural networks using the networks inside the brain as the model. He's the godfather of artificial intelligence, and he's coming next week to talk here.

So, with computers developing so fast, back in the 70s, I thought, wonderful, computers will allow exactly what you mentioned. You can assemble huge amounts of information, put it into the computer, and that will allow you to go along paths and connect things which you couldn't do with the human brain. You've got a bit of information in a book here, a bit of information in an interview there, you've got a photograph over there – the human brain can't consciously bring these things together, but you can put them into a computer and then you can ask questions, and then the computer makes the links between them. I worked with several brilliant computer scientists, one of whom implemented the new form of computer system which was based on the idea that a computer can think in a fuzzy way. So, you don't have to get the question absolutely right. You put in a question, the system gives you some kind of answer, and then you feed back to the system information to say, this is good and that is not such a good answer – the system then looks at your question again and gives you a better answer because it took the feedback into account. It's a human-aided artificial intelligence.

I was working with the pioneer who first wrote that program in Cambridge, and I thought for a long time that what I'll do is I'll build up a big library: I'll go to lots of places, take lots of photographs, and if I accumulate a huge amount of information inside my computer, then I'll be able to do new things. It certainly helped, and one thing the computer certainly did for me is, it forced me to think about what I was looking for when I put things into it because I had to decide, this is rubbish, that is good. There's an old saying – GIGO – which means 'garbage in, garbage out'. If you don't put good things into the computer, you won't get anything good out of it. So, it forced me to think carefully.

But what I tended to find in several of my projects is that by the time I'd finished putting all the information into the computer, I already knew the answers. My brain was better, though the computer certainly helped me discipline it. On the one hand, you're absolutely right, I can do all sorts of things that I could never have done 10 or 20 years ago. I can look up a theory or find a photograph, so data searching is much more efficient than it was before. There are many paths I can go along which I couldn't have gone along before. But when it comes to *understanding*, then the computer doesn't replace my ability to move outside narrow categories or to think about questions which other people haven't perhaps thought about so much – *here*, in the human brain; it's not in the data.

What I do now is I read a lot and put a lot in the computer. Then I put it on one side, and, as you do as an artist, I just speak, or I just write. And deep inside me – all the work has been done deep inside me – it then comes out in a pattern which often is very surprising. It is one of the delights of being a creative writer, that you sit down in the morning, and you think, what shall I write about today? Well, I'll write about beauty. Now if you said to me, what do you know about beauty, I'd say I know nothing about it. But when I start writing about beauty, bits of poetry come into my mind. 'Beauty is truth, truth beauty.' And I suddenly find that I know a considerable amount about beauty. I've been thinking about it in the back of my mind for years. So, I either speak it or write it. At the end of the day, I've written five pages on beauty, and then my wife says to me, what were you working on today? And I say, I was writing about beauty. She says, what did you write? And I say, I have no idea; I'll have to read it tomorrow to see what I think about it because it's there, but I've lost it. It's come up from a deeper level onto the page.

I think every human being is constantly surprised at how much they know. If you talk to children, for example Zilan's son James – you'd ask him something, and you'd be constantly surprised at how much he understands and knows, once you assume that he's an intelligent human being. Even very small children know a great deal.

To summarise, digitalisation and the computer are very useful tools. They can be likened to a car –without the car you can't get many places, but the car can't do anything without you. *You* have to decide what you're going to do with it. So, all this digitisation is a very useful tool to make certain things possible that weren't possible before. But beyond that it's all been *here* (points to his head).

TY: That's wonderful.

I think every place has a different spirit because of geographic location. The culture grows and develops in the context of its geography. In your work you have studied how ancient societies continually influence the future. How do you feel about a map of the spiritual world? Are there patterns? I mean the effects of geography on behaviour, just like we are now talking about the differences between East and West.

AM: Are you asking about the spiritual world or about the patterns of cultures?

TY: Patterns of cultures.

AM: This has been what I'm most interested in, particularly over the last ten or fifteen years. In fact, I've just done a short talk on patterns of culture because one of my YouTube followers requested it, particularly with reference to being an anthropologist.

In the middle of the 20th century there were two women anthropologists in America, Margaret Mead and Ruth Benedict, who were very influential. They were wonderful anthropologists and grand theorists. Ruth Benedict wrote a book called *Patterns of Culture*. She divided the world into two forms of culture, Apollonian and Dionysian. Apollonian valued restraint and calm; Dionysian valued excess. Then Benedict applied the theory to Japan. She wrote one of the very best books on Japan because she caught many of the contradictions. The title of the book, *The Chrysanthemum and the Sword: Patterns of Japanese Culture*, catches the big contradiction in Japan: the chrysanthemum, which is a beautiful flower – and the sword. What was particularly outstanding about her book was that she wrote it without going to Japan. She did it by interviewing Japanese prisoners of war in America because she wrote it for the American army, so they could understand better the people whom they were fighting. It's a brilliant book, and Benedict had the idea that Japan had a pattern. Now in a lot of academic work you have to know that something exists before you can find it. It's like Columbus going to America: you have to know there's something there, and then you can make the voyage.

The first thing with a lot of my work is having developed confidence that there are patterns to cultures. It's a principle of anthropologists. They do it on a micro scale: this tribe here has one pattern to its culture, that tribe there has another pattern. They've always assumed that each society will have a pattern, but they tend to do it in a confined way. There was a great American anthropologist, a man called A.L. Kroeber. He was a world thinker, and he addressed civilisations. My development has been to the level above countries, to the concept of a civilisation. A civilisation is a set of people who are united in some way. They don't necessarily live together, but they usually have a common language, common assumptions, philosophies, sometimes nationality. If you think of the world at a civilisational level, there are probably eight or nine (I've written about four of them in one of my books). It was the idea behind Huntington's book on *The Clash of Civilizations*.

I believe that each civilisation has a pattern: it's not a culture but a civilisation. If you use certain methods which have been developed by great thinkers like Tocqueville, Montesquieu, Adam Smith and others, they believed that you could look at a whole place like China. If you look at China as a civilisation, it has a pattern and quite a simple one. In fact, one of the curious theories I came up with recently is that the larger and the older the civilisation, the simpler it has to be. If you take a little place like England, which is quite recent, around a thousand years, it is very complicated. If you take China – three-four thousand years, vast in geographical space and diverse – if it was complicated, it would all fall into pieces. China you can explain on six or seven principles: language, imperial system and so on. Once you have that, the whole civilisation holds together. America is the same. It's very big, and Tocqueville in his great book on America said it's a very simple place. Anyone can understand America in two weeks: liberty, fraternity, equality – and money and religion – that's it. Whereas Denmark or Holland are small and incredibly complicated; it's counterintuitive.

I do believe in patterns of cultures, and I believe more and more that, where there are clashes of civilisations in our world, if we can explain to people so that they understand the differences between civilisations, we can live together. If you just reject a whole civilisation, as many people in this country do when they just think, China's awful or Russia's awful or America's awful, then we will have more and more confrontation and conflict. That's my answer.

My turn to ask a question. This one is from a Chinese student friend of mine, Shuo, who lives in Shanghai and whom I've known for 10-12 years now. The first one is about what you've sort of talked about: in what ways is the traditional culture of Hong Kong, Taiwan Province and Mainland China different from each other?

TY: Hong Kong, I think, doesn't have a fixed tradition. When I was younger, I kept trying to find out where we came from in

Hong Kong and how we developed. I loved European and American things. I went to Europe to travel there and see it for myself, and to find answers. When I came back, I started learning more about Chinese culture, though it was difficult to find information about it. My friends were Westernised, but I wanted to go back to the Chinese origins. Not just to become symbolically Chinese, but to know where I came from. That's what brought me to Taiwan Province later, because in Taiwan Province there is a lot of traditional culture. Hong Kong is a bit like Chinatown. Not in the sense of being high or low, that's not it at all. But it's about living somewhere not governed by you. So, you have to be strong. The image of hero in Hong Kong is always a kind of tragic hero like in John Woo's *A Better Tomorrow*. Hong Kong talks about heroes a lot. You have to achieve everything by yourself. You have to be strong. You have to have friends. This kind of energy. I think Hong Kong has a strong drive to understand the world and to build a definition of themselves. That makes them clever, aggressive and fast-talking. They are sophisticated and deliberate. They don't do too much or too little. Hong Kong is very fast.

As for Taiwan, I lived there for over 10 years, and Taiwan Province bears an imprint of constant changes of government. Every time new parties come along, and things change again and again. Because of that the tendency is to be relaxed and happy in the moment. It's like, I'm happy, and I'm enjoying today. Everything is temporary. Nothing is long term. Taiwan Province was influenced a lot by Japanese high culture. They are very polite and cultured. And they are nice people. That's my impression of Taiwan Province.

China is undergoing a big change now. The country as a whole is booming, and the individual people too see progress in their life conditions, but not everybody has improved to the same extent. The Chinese are looking for new identity. And to present a unified front of their new identity. They want to learn more and to get more. This gives the young generation some freedom.

AM: So, in a way Hong Kong and Mainland China are more alike, in what you described. Because they are both looking for more and wanting...

TY: Mainland China has a big idea of togetherness. And they want to be showing what they are now.

AM: Projecting themselves.

TY: Yes. Hong Kong is more careful, more mature. But really fast.

AM: Good. I will pass that on to my Shanghai friend.

TY: When I was younger, I created a map in the format person-time-place. For instance, I would have an entry like 'Picasso, 1930s, France'. I used this map as a tool for organising my thoughts and impressions from the art I saw. There were no computers yet, so I did all this manually. I thought that by looking at the origins, at when and where an artist worked, I could see deeper into the physical and spiritual sides of their art. You said that you were interested in databases and that you built a similar kind of map for your work. I would like to learn more about your system.

AM: For many years, my wife and I were trying to use computers to help us in our research, and it took some years to realise that all information can basically be arranged by a small number of simple categories. In our query system we, of course, have free-text searching, but in terms of what's known as Boolean or structured searching categories, we have time, place, person, medium and source. In other words, when we're searching in one of our databases, I want to see a certain person in a certain place on a certain day in a photograph or in a film or in another medium. The fifth one we sometimes need is the source, e.g., the reference in a certain book and the page number that talks about the subject of the query. With those four or five criteria, you can search for almost anything. It fixes everything together.

The second thing to say is that increasingly I've realised that to understand human beings, you have to have the intersection of time and space. That's why my life has been going backwards and forwards between the two big disciplines that deal with space and time.

History deals with time. I don't think you can understand anything out of time. Part of an explanation is always what happened up to then. There are many people in my discipline of anthropology who go to China and think they can understand China without knowing its history. That's ridiculous. History is everywhere in China: even if it's not physically there, it's there mentally. You have to be a historian to understand your present world and the future.

But if you're *just* a historian and you just understand time, you tend to only work on a particular country because you can't understand the whole world in time just like that. So, you tend to be a specialist on France or China or England. And then you lose the dimension of space because you can't understand China unless you look at America or France or the rest of the world. You need to have both the comparison with space dimension and the comparison in the time depth. When you put those two things together and look at human beings within that, you begin to understand them both comparatively to someone in another culture and someone in a different period.

This picks up on something you said earlier, I think. You said that young people today know a great deal more and they're much more flexible in their thoughts. That's all true. But at the same time, they know a lot less about certain things. Even our children, and certainly our grandchildren, know little about the history of this country in the way that I do. I was meeting a young relative, and he's studying history at school and wants to become a historian. I asked him, what history do you study at school? He said, Queen Elizabeth I (that is 40 years in the 16th century) and the Cold War. I asked, well, what about the Industrial Revolution, the Scientific Revolution, the Renaissance? No-no, he said, we don't do that. We just do these two particular things for exams, as though they were not connected in any way. If you went out in the street and asked people a very simple question, like how old is Cambridge University, or how did universities start, or what is the purpose of a university historically, most of them wouldn't know much about that or even the larger history of England.

The Chinese are better educated in our history than we are. Indeed, I've always been amazed when I talk to Chinese sschoolchildren: they know more about the history of the West than most Westerners do. They know about Western philosophies. You know, in a lecture in China, I can say to schoolchildren, can you tell me something about the ideas of Adam Smith or Montesquieu or John Stuart Mill – and they say, yes-yes, we are taught that. Here they probably wouldn't know the first thing about them.

On the other hand, young people's minds are filled with things that I know nothing about. This is demonstrated in our culture when we play games with our children. At Christmas or on festivities, we often stop and play a game, a general knowledge game, where you ask the other team questions. My wife and I never play now because they say, name the singer in this latest pop record or who won the Eurovision song contest two years ago. They have a whole layer of understanding which we don't have, and their minds are filled with as much information and knowledge, but it doesn't overlap very much with my world. Anyway, that's an aside.

So... time and space. You need both and then you have the humans in the middle of it.

TY: Wonderful.

In whatever we do, we can be active or reactive. Maybe in the academic world it is like that too. Certain views of history and other things were built up for a long time and became established, and now in powerful institutions like Cambridge there is a lot of questioning of these older established views. I wonder how academic work is going to change because people now are at another level of knowledge. Previously academia was powerful and dictated a certain way of asking questions and giving answers. But now more and more people, including academics, are using different, sometimes more spiritual ways to understand things, and they are working in a more attentive, detailed way. A new kind of understanding is developing. How will academia change? And not just academia, but education as well. What will the future be moving to?

AM: There are two questions here: one is education, the other what the future will move to. On the education side, I haven't been in that lately: I retired some years ago.

But I suspect that two different sorts of movements are occurring. One is specialisation: every discipline now has so much more information, and you get down more and more detail. Looking at what my colleagues talk about in their lectures and seminars in my discipline of anthropology and also in history, you see that people have become more and more specialised. They are the specialists on some sub-aspect of some sub-aspect – unchallenged, and no one can knock them off. But the overarching grand visions of anthropology when I was learning it, talking about the whole world, and about humanity and human beings – no one would do that now. They would say, but what about people walking up and down the street in front of King's College on a certain day? I'm doing my thesis on that. What are they wearing in front of King's College on a certain day? That's my Ph.D. So, there's a micro tendency.

On the other hand, the world is now globally interconnected; there are many people from different cultures and civilisations, and films and art and everything has become globalised. I've noticed that a lot of my younger colleagues are also very broad. The disciplinary boundaries between subjects have become much weaker, and people move between subjects. When we have new people coming to King's College as researchers, I ask them what discipline they're in. In the past they would say, I'm a chemist, or, I'm a physicist. Now they say, I'm a molecular, computational, biological, chemical cosmologist. This is quite a healthy thing because when you're pursuing a problem you have to forget disciplinary boundaries, and this is something I like about your work.

You're interested in trying to understand and to communicate certain things. If this takes you into film or opera or photography or writing, it doesn't matter. You pursue it using whatever tools are available, whereas traditionally the discipline imposed a boundary, and you couldn't pursue the question any further. There's a saying in history: 'study topics, not periods'. In other words, pursue a problem and then it doesn't matter whether it takes you outside your special period. I think simultaneously everyone's getting narrower and narrower and also wider and wider in certain ways.

As for the question about the future, I've written a book called *How Can We Survive?* I've taken eight subjects like work, artificial intelligence, disease, population, ecology, education and explained how we've got to where we are now and then said, this is the problem we're facing with global warming or loss of work because of artificial intelligence. This is our problem. Once you know what the problem is, you can solve it. It's not very difficult. The difficult thing is to understand your predicament in the present. Then you give your solutions. The last quarter or third of each of my essays is saying, this is what we should do about it.

For example, health and disease. The big problem in the world, in Britain, for example, is that we have lost control of disease because of several things. One is aging. We have large numbers of elderly people who have to be medically supported at a huge cost that increases and increases and increases. Because of diagnosis, almost everyone is ill. When you get statistics for health in this country, about a quarter of the people think they are ill with some disease. They are going to their doctors and wanting medicines and treatment. That, combined with the increasing cost of medicine and cures, means that our expenditure on health is going up steeply, and we just can't afford it. That is the problem in much of the developed world, the spiralling costs.

The solution is quite simple, and it is based on China's period during Chairman Mao: barefoot doctors. If you remember what China did, it didn't have any money and it didn't have any doctors. So, it trained teams of people in simple diagnosis of common illnesses, equipped them with basic medical instruments and pills and tonics for common illnesses and sent them off to go from village to village. This was amazingly effective. I did the same when I worked in a village in Nepal. They didn't have a hospital or a health post, but I used to go out every year with ten different medicines, for coughs and thorns and very simple things. I could deal with about 80-90% of the things that were troubling them. If it was serious, then they had to go out to see a doctor.

I've seen this done in China now, where you go to a village and you have a local health post with a partly qualified, easily educated person with a computer, and he or she deals with 90% of all the problems. If they're more serious, people go to a local hospital. So, you take away from the 19th-century tendency to put everyone in hospitals and to use very expensive, long-trained doctors (around eight years), and you empower local people to deal with almost all the local health problems.

My next question is very broad. If you had to summarise the deeper questions behind all your work, what is it you are ultimately searching for?

TY: I think I'm searching for the way of the energy. We still know the world by matter. We touch and feel and learn about the story of different things and why they are here – it's all very physical. But now it's becoming complicated, and people are thinking about dreams and the material world and thinking how to repackage the knowledge of what we see and what we feel. Also, quantum mechanics came along, and there are questions about whether a thing exists before you thought about it or exists because you think about it, and what is the relationship between thoughts and things, and what are the possibilities when we are looking at things. Previously our education presented looking at things as simply, yes, OK, we look at things. But now the when and the how of this looking become important too, and we have to put looking in a context because what we see through looking is affected by the context in which our looking takes place. That's why when looking at a painting and seeing it as good, I ask who is looking at it. It's not just who painted it, but also how it is being looked at. I think this is an important question for today's commercialised world because when a large number of people, 'the market', says yes to something, who is it that is saying yes? Not the attentive people, certainly. They keep quiet and don't participate in mass trends. There is always a kind of noise coming from the public, from people who are not really paying attention to the questions asked and the answers given. And because of this noise you start believing in numbers. I think it is a problem. I think this is the downfall of all this public art – they are looking for mass reaction. One very important thing is the uselessness of art. There must be no function. When it has function, it becomes another thing. Having no function helps with balancing.

AM: What about architecture? Architecture has a function. You have a building, and yet...

TY: That's a good question, but architecture can be put into another category. We began from caves and roof-like things provided by nature which we used to shield ourselves from rain and other things. Then we started to build structures for ourselves by trying to imitate nature. Afterwards you have sculpture, you have painting, and when the crisis comes, a human face is put on the universe. Because all this is really the point of view of humans looking at the world. This world is made by humans. Buddha talked about nothingness, but they put a face on Buddha. Religions go through a spiritual period in the beginning, and they always get to a stage where things like heaven and hell are given a look of human beings. They put these images in the building and give meaning to the structure of the building, to the various parts of it. The ceremony is given a function. Later, in the time of the Renaissance, everything becomes individual, designed by people. Celebrating humans. This includes Baroque. After Baroque we gradually modernised. Bauhaus changed a lot. Art Deco and Art Nouveau cut more and more, and art came down to earth more and more. And afterwards it moved to geometry. These tendencies are already in Bauhaus in 1930s, I think. Later Tadao Ando brought the Eastern thinking of space to churches and other buildings. A lot changed again. Zaha Hadid used the computer to design her curved buildings. Though I think her system will develop into a meta-universe. She already had problems reconciling the curved shapes with the functional side of the buildings. They are curved on the outside but square on the inside. I think architecture is closely related to what we believe at the time. But I also believe that architecture has spirit, because of proportions. The temples in Athens have very good proportions. Proportion is a mystery of the human perceptive mind that sees in everything proportions contained in a human being. They start with human proportions, then separate them to look at nature, but keeping in mind the relative scale. I think the most important thing is this proportion is related to our scale. It's all from the perspective of human eyes. If humans were bigger, maybe all those things would have been different.

AM: Thank you. Earlier you spoke about the influence of Buddhism on your work. What about the influence of Daoism?

TY: I'm not really a fan of *Dao De Jing*. I just get the simple things about things not sitting on the ground but floating in the air. That's what I believe in Daoism, the constant need to balance. Everything is floating, yin-yang, always balancing and rebalancing. Things are constantly reflected in one another. What we see as one thing in this moment, in the next moment disappears because it's a collection of reflections from other things. Everything is both a reflection and a mirror of other things. Everything is always together, floating. So, a central thing for Daoism is to see what is right now. Nothing is fixed by history or by facts. Many things coexist, and what we see is affected by the many reflections.

Daoism speaks of emptiness, but that's another way of saying that everything is there at once. If you walk in a room with 100 people and you know just one of them, you go up to them and say hello, and you might think it's something. But when you know all 100, you will see nothing and everything at once. It's not the same thing as arrogantly saying that you know everything. In this multi-perceptual state, the endless multiple reflecting is drawing you deeper and deeper every instant. To me creativity is the ability to see from different angles. There is no need to create anything. Everything is already present here. Staying in balance and seeing everything at once means you can see several angles at the same time, you can see your own transparency, the structure, the colours, the weight. And you see that all this is changeable by just altering the way of seeing, that nothing is inherent. So, when I 'tune' into emptiness, I can feel at once how heavy, what's the colour, what's the reflection, what's the texture, who put it there. Everything at once. Like the distribution of energy inside an atom is formed by many different energies superimposing. Even the simplest thing on Earth is a superposition of many, many reflections. So, when the Chinese talk, sometimes poetically, about the reflections on water in the morning, they are talking about the same thing. About how to feel the world.

AM: Fascinating. I have more questions, but it's your turn to ask.

TY: I received a big insight about science from you when you said that laboratory science goes through many possibilities in a short period of time to find the one which is better. I also have an impression that the English were spiritual in ancient times. For example, they built Stonehenge, and it's not very far from London. But later London became very educated and organised. What is the relationship between these? How did these two very different ways get along?

AM: What do you mean by 'spiritual' in this case?

TY: I mean they believed in something beyond matter.

AM: The simple answer is that there was a big break. The people who built Stonehenge, the early Druids and people who inhabited Britain right up to the time the Romans came, were possibly related to the Celtic people, the people in Scotland, Ireland, north of France and so on, who are still spiritual. They believe in spirits, witches and things above matter. For long thousands of years of history this country had people like that, with a very spiritual view on things. Then the Romans came, and they didn't completely eliminate it, but they suppressed it to a large extent.

Then you had the invasion of people from northern Germany and Denmark, the Anglo-Saxons. There's something very peculiar about the Anglo-Saxons. Their mythology and their folklore are of the kind which influenced Wagner, for instance; he's basically using the Northern myths. *The Lord of the Rings* by Tolkien is based on Anglo-Saxon mythology. They do believe in mythical things which you can't easily see, in a spirit world of a kind. But that kind of world is very different from the one that you find in truly spiritual places like Japan or China or even Celtic cultures, because they are tales and legends about heroes, dragons and that sort of things, but you know they are stories. You wouldn't expect to meet them. They're not just around you. What is characteristic of the Anglo-Saxon world is that it's very practical and this-worldly. We do have stories we tell our children about fairies and magical things, but they are stories for children. When you are grown up, you live in what sociologists like to call a 'disenchanted world'.

Many people think this was caused by the Reformation, when the English broke away from the Catholic Church and Catholicism which has some of that magic in it. The Reformation did make it more extreme in a place like Cambridge, which was an early Reformation city. The last little vestiges of a world where nature, the physical world and the spiritual world are linked together, so at any moment you are dealing simultaneously with the material and the spiritual, disappeared.

If you hold up a cup and say to Japanese, what is this, they would at the same time see a cup and a spirit which is in it, a *kami*. It's not just a physical object. Now that world where spirit and matter are interfused was more or less absent among the Anglo-Saxons. I've only recently been thinking about it, but what was it about these people who were fishermen and hunters and kept cattle, and who seemed to have developed over thousands of years a kind of mental world which had already separated out spirit and matter? The Reformation was just the final stage in that.

A good place to look is in literature. You have stories in Anglo-Saxon and early medieval literature which tell about monsters, for example *Beowulf*, and the sort of stories you get in Tolkien, but you don't get any feeling anywhere that the world is enchanted. If you take one of our great classics written in the 14th century by Geoffrey Chaucer, *The Canterbury Tales* (a collection of stories different people are telling about their life) – it's all here and now, absolutely no hint of anything else.

Another classic example is Shakespeare. If you look at his works, 90% of them are just here and now: history plays and so on. Occasionally there's a bit of fantasy: if you go to Scotland you have *Macbeth* and the witches – well, that's up in Scotland. His only fantasy plays with some sort of spirits and so on are dreams. You have *A Midsummer Night's Dream*. It's called *A Midsummer Night's Dream*: it's not true, it's a dream. It's more like a Kunqu opera. And the other is *The Tempest*, which is a fantasy set on an island separated from the world. Right at the end the magician gives a speech saying it was all made up. It's all a dream – don't believe any of it. So, even Shakespeare contains his fantasy in his two great plays about it. Otherwise, it's all here and now, practical – and all our great playwrights are like that.

The English may think, well, we must have believed in that once and then it disappeared. An extreme example of this is during the Romantic movement in poetry. If you look at the English Romantic poets – Wordsworth, Keats, Shelley, Coleridge, Byron, Blake – they all say, once, when we were children, we believed in enchantment and were filled with spirit, before the modern scientific world shattered it all and so on. But as a historian, as I go back I see that this was not the case.

And so, what you see in London now is an efficient, disenchanted, world. The elements of anything like enchantment are coming in from people like you and Akram Khan. Such people come from fantastical worlds; they bring this enchantment to London and enrich the art and thought here. But the people who are here – the natives, so to speak – don't necessarily believe any of it.

TY: They seemed to combine spirit and science, I think. They had an integrated view of both together. Alchemy, for example.

AM: Yes, they had astrology, which is telling the fortune or reading from the stars. And alchemy, which is turning base metals like iron into gold. Newton, though a great scientist, believed in those things. He wrote about them, and he believed in them too. In each case there's no spirit involved. What they're saying is that there are forces which we can't understand and which we can harness. In alchemy you don't believe that there is any kind of spirit. You believe that there are hidden laws in nature which you don't understand, and it produces an outcome which you want. It's the same with the stars. They aren't spirits. They are forces up there. It's like Feng Shui. There are forces of the winds, waters, stars, whatever, which can help you foretell the future or determine your character or turn things into other things. It's a marginal case. It isn't an enchanted world, but it is a world which has many things which we don't understand, and which affect our lives. That has always been true, and many people believe in that still. Most newspapers will have predictions about how the day you were born will affect you and so on.

Popular beliefs of that kind, astrological and so on, are compatible with science. 'Science' is a difficult word to define. Many people think of laboratory science when you say 'science', and they think of Bacon, Newton and so on. It's better to use the word in the Continental meaning, from the word *scientia* which means 'knowledge' in Latin.

Some of my scientific friends used to say you mustn't use the word 'science' – you should use the expression 'reliable knowledge'. If you have reliable knowledge that the bus will come at a certain time, that is science. It just means a certainty of some kind, predictability, repeatability. Much of our life is scientific. Children are wonderful scientists because they have to learn the patterns of predictability and reliable knowledge. If a child doesn't acquire reliable knowledge about fire, falling off things and so on, they will be dead. So, children become scientists. They do the guessing and testing that all scientists do. They build up a huge store of 'reliable knowledge'. My mother, if hungry, will be angry; once she's eaten a meal, she'll be fine – that's reliable knowledge.

Let me ask you a question. I think we've talked about it a bit, but it would be nice to expand it. I know you are interested in the New Orientalism. Oversimplifying what I remember of what you said, you basically meant that you wanted to renew or bring back a vision of the world which was present in China two or three thousand years ago. Have I got it right or is there more to it than that?

TY: I always develop my work from within. It's not like I study many different materials and have art coming up from that. For many years I wrote my detailed notes, like a meditation, and I've gathered these notes in a number of notebooks. My published books contain material from these notebooks. When I was writing these notes, I'd have a long period of time when I thought about nothing, and the words formed and came up from there. Once the words came up, I would jot them down. I didn't plan or research anything deliberately. I had the books by my side, and when I had questions, I read the books, but I didn't immediately write anything. I left it and sometime afterwards I would suddenly think of some things connecting together, and I made a note of that. My notes and my system grew organically from within me. I'm not saying that I'm a Daoist because maybe I'm different from the definitions that have been put on Daoism, but when I look at Daoist teachings, I find they give me information. I find Buddhism is more open because I'm receptive to space and I sense that we are here and not here at the same time. So, we can feel the whole space at once. There is no need to be limited by where we are or by looking at details. I've used that for a long time in different works, so it's already inside me. I'm not someone who reads a lot about Daoism, but I understand some of the words. I would remember, oh they say that, and suddenly everything is...

AM: What about *Yi Jing*?

TY: *Yi Jing* for me is... too practical. It has so many symbols. I worry that it makes things complicated. You know, they have one thing in China, and maybe not just in China, but in the East: they don't like words. When you know too many words, you get stuck in them. So, when we feel enough, we don't read anything. When I have a doubt or a hesitation about something and can't find a solution, I read something. But I'm not reading to make me understand. My teacher gave me good advice once. Paraphrased in English, it means, 'when you're passing a door, don't go in if you don't need to'. There can be different situations. Sometimes you want to know something, and you go to the library, find the books and a summary or meaning of everything. But this is the way to do it if you need to. If you're not feeling that, don't go in. Maybe in your mind you have another place to go. When you try to go in and learn everything, you'll be stuck. So, come out, ask a question and note it down. Maybe there are ten chapters in the book, but the time hasn't come yet for you to read the ninth chapter. Maybe that time will come in five years. So, don't go to the ninth chapter. Go to the second chapter because the time is right for it, read the second chapter and stop. The message we get from reading is according to our energy. If it's not yet strong enough, you will not receive the message.

Sometimes I read something, and I feel, oh, this is not quite true. I was reading a collection of the most important Buddhist poetry, and there it said very directly, 'everything is nothing'. This was an

Indian work translated during the Tang dynasty. The translation was beautiful, with elaborate words. But that's not the Indian way. It's an Eastern tendency to give you a saying, and *boom!* – you immediately understand everything. This *boom!* isn't the Indian way. In the Indian way, you get a teaching, and you ask a question. When you get an answer to that question, you keep asking questions. You ask everyone you meet in the street or under the trees, someone gives you an answer, and with that you find how to make the next step. It's very different from the Chinese way. When I'm not held captive by words, maybe I can see more. But I keep asking different people to make sure I'm not going in a false way. Dao, I think, is a way of looking at things forever. I look outside and see a building. Then I look behind the building to see what's there. And then behind that thing, and the thing behind it. I'll see very far like that. It's the way of stages: where we are, what we are thinking, what is our level. From there we find the balance. When we find the balance, don't try to artificially get more than that.

AM: Well, this will be my last question for today. Lots of people are very interested in the fact that I'm interviewing you. They say, can you begin to explain what Tim Yip is like, who he is? And I say, well, sometimes I feel, having worked in Nepal among shamans, that he is a reborn, very early shaman from the 6th - 7th century BC, come back into the world to bring back that kind of knowledge.

The feature of Siberian and other shamans is that, as the natural world and the spiritual world are fused together, the shamans become, in certain kinds of shamanism, messengers or communicators between worlds. They are like a radio receiver: their ancestors and spirits come into them. And often, in some versions, shamans go into trance, and then they speak in spirit voices. That's the full form of shamanism, but many shamans don't actually go into trance. Still, they feel that there are messages coming into them and they act as the communicators of these messages.

Now, I think all artists feel this, that they are overcome with a power which is greater than themselves or they're not sure where where it comes from. But in your case, looking at some of your artwork, it seems very similar to what a shaman does. As in my case in Nepal, what a shaman does is that they do their ritual, and they assemble all sorts of special objects, special foods and special smells. And then they go through a series of actions, which is the ritual, but they also recite their myths and stories telling what this or that ingredient of the ritual is. And then, as the ritual builds up, they may go into trance.

So, if we looked at your films and your art displays as a form of shamanic ritual, would we be very wrong in thinking that?

TY: It's not wrong, it's something like... People have different gifts. When I was born, I too had some gifts from other dimensions. They affected what I did in life. From the beginning, I had idealistic kinds of goals for my life, searching for something intensely. It's a feeling from within. If you look at my work with traditional designs, I don't directly copy the tradition. I change some things and sometimes even connect with the contemporary. I don't know why this happens. But I know where to put which element and what's the angle. My painting, for example, is very fast. I suddenly know where and how to put the lines to express this or that face. Each face is different. Different lines to add. Or I set up the colours in the movie in such a way that you can feel the emotion of the movie.

And even with actors. I might be working with an actor who has never done a period film and has only done modern films. But when they see the costume I made for their character, they can feel how to walk in that costume and how to show the features of the costume. They feel inspired by the costume, even though I always make big complex costumes, and it's difficult for the actor. They have to show the beauty. They have to walk in it, with big tails and other things. It all becomes part of the performance. The Chinese have a gift of relating everything to dance, to movement, to the meaning of the move. Every costume is like that. Costumes express the meaning of the movie in their own way, and I research and study a lot to achieve that, to use form to create emotion. It's like when you are watching *Crouching Tiger, Hidden Dragon*, you see Yu Shu Lien's costume is designed with sort of double sleeves. In the scene where she is fighting with two swords, the sleeves accentuate her mastery. Details like that are already in me from somewhere.

When Ang Lee talked about how he made a film, he said he first of all came up with images. Maybe for *Crouching Tiger* he saw two women; or a man and a woman high up among bamboo trees. Then he created the whole movie around these images. That's why I worked with him so well in that film. For example, even in normal scenes with two key characters talking, I set up the buildings and the scene overall in such a way that it looks as if the characters are suspended in large space. There are many scenes that show big spaces with the characters in the middle, as if they are floating in the space. All this is preparation for flying later in the film. Also, the scenes with the large open space and two people fighting in it have a psychological dimension.

Some of this I learned from Surrealism and the modern language of art. A lot came from contemporary art and things translated into contemporary art from classical art. I tried to find the identity of the earlier forms and how they translated the representation of dreamlike fighting by reforming the understanding of light, colours and other elements. This helped me to go back to the Oriental kind of tradition and to connect the two together, so that I can do something that Western people will understand. They are familiar with colours. They may not know their cultural symbolism, but they can feel.

I believe that everything has a second language. Second language is not knowledge. But you feel it. By arranging visual elements in a certain way, or by grouping or separating them, I can make the audience laugh or cry. When you are watching the film, it seems as if everything is normal and nothing special is going on in the scene, but there is a lot of work I have to do beforehand for the audience to feel that way. I have to find the language first and arrange everything to follow that language and become normal. When you watch for five minutes, you don't walk away – you believe my logic. Maybe I set up all the windows to be big. Or maybe everyone is in the shadows. Or everyone is wearing big elaborate costumes that are different from what historical knowledge tells us. You watch five minutes of that, and you accept it. Everything becomes…

AM: Normal.

TY: Yes. I think this is already set up by the contemporary culture because they try to get a global audience. So, they try to combine many different shapes, forms, colours, patterns. After that they would re-shape it into a style, and modern people will see it and think, oh, it's really interesting and new. Because culture makes a difference – culture has a rhythm inside. Unlike modern Hollywood movies, where they don't add any real culture. They just mix arbitrarily. But we don't like looking at something like that. We want to see the volumes of the culture, the real power of these colours, lines and other elements. We want to sense the beauty. Now colours are everywhere, with wrong colours being put side by side and mixed in a way that changes their identity. It's because they want to build up something new, but this kind of new is just for one second. The things I want to make are new forever. Everything can go into a flow of colour relationships again. Everything can be reborn. We feel the origin, and this makes us feel more deeply, inspiring our senses to a higher level. That's why we make movies. That's why we make art.

But the modern commercial market condenses a large mass of shallow likes and dislikes into the opinion of the mass market. Everything is pastel. Everything is flat. They have no new things. They become more and more similar, and the only criterion is whether it's good in the opinion of the mass market. Creating or reforming the culture is difficult. Chaotic or organic or unexpected can be brought in to form multiple layers of the existence of things, so that it's not a matter of catching what is right or wrong. There are many layers, and my work is controlling and modifying these layers to give people things they would like. But by making them see real things, get the path to the origin, and also get new inspiration. Inspiration is good energy. It's not something flat. It's real meaning.

There are two questions I'd like to ask. I read your books with a lot of interest. On the one hand, you are a very serious scholar. On the other hand, you always speak of a mysterious inner world. A world of myths and magic. You are like a pilgrim walking higher and higher up a mountain to see things in different ways. Ways in which other people don't see. You are deeply moved by Eastern art. You wrote *Letters to Lily*. These things are outside your professional sphere, but something within you makes you want to go in these directions. Your own world. Your openness. Your imagination. Maybe it comes from the loneliness of your childhood, when nobody understood you, but you had another world that kept you going. Is it still there? Is there still this other world within, urging you on? And the other question is, in your opinion, how do people see things differently after reading your books?

AM: So, the influence *on* my work and the influence *of* my work...

The last person who understands their work is the artist. I don't understand mine; I need someone to tell me. If I was a psychologist looking at me, I would say... 'Well, he wasn't particularly talented as an intellectual at school. He was just middle of the road and teachers thought he was middling. And he went on like that until towards the end of his time at Oxford. People said he's a little bit better and he could be an academic or something. But there was nothing special there.'

And indeed, if you look at quite a lot of my historical and anthropological work until I wrote *Letters to Lily*, it was good, and people liked it, and I got promotions and so on. But there was not much breaking away from what a good academic does. And then, around the time of writing *Letters to Lily* and one or two other books, I went in another direction, which was to try and write much more freely, in a relaxed way and using my imagination much more.

As a child I was told again and again, 'Your writing is rather wooden. You think it all out and put the arguments there, but you don't use your imagination very much.' And it was really when I started to trust myself and to think, well, it doesn't matter now, I'll write what I want to write and I'll ask the questions that I really want answers to, not the questions which my colleagues think are important, that I became much more relaxed and free.

There was also the matter of style because if you write academic work, you're trapped in certain conventions of expressing yourself in a rather complex manner because you're trying to carry on complex arguments. You use a certain amount of jargon, footnotes, write in longish sentences with a complex grammatical structure. But I was increasingly interested in the writing of people I admired, like George Orwell and some of the great English essay writers, earlier writers who wrote very simply. They used Anglo-Saxon words, no Latinisms. They didn't use sub-clauses. They wrote more or less as they spoke, and that made it more direct. But in that case, you had to really know what you wanted to say as you were writing or as you were speaking. I think that's a matter of age and experience because by the time I was writing like this I was sixty or so and I had a large store of experience. I didn't need to read a new book on this or that. I had been thinking about it and I explored the world and travelled. So, I could just write simply and clearly.

Writing is a very curious business. It must be similar to what you do because when I sit down with my pen, I don't know what I'm going to write. And yet it comes out, and my mind is only just ahead of what I'm writing. But it's also far ahead of it because one talent which I've developed, partly in relation to filmmaking, is the ability to take any subject and then talk about it at a reasonable level without hesitations and deviations and keep an audience interested.

I've just done 250 of these little talks, and when people look at them, they really like them. Not many people could do that, if you say to them, well, just pick an arbitrary subject, anything, like a camera or the lights or this croissant. (Picks up a croissant from the table.) If you said, Alan, talk for five minutes about a croissant, I could easily talk.

I'd say, well, this is typical French: a lot of outer exterior, nothing inside – empty! We British, we have *solid* bread, we don't have this sort of stuff. It's also typically French because it's the sort of insubstantial stuff that the French have for breakfast. We British have a solid breakfast. So, the whole national character of the British and the French can be read off a croissant.

So, you see, I can talk about anything – which my friends complain about... When that ability combines with free writing, you sometimes feel inspired, as I was trying to describe when I was talking about shamans. Someone asked W.B. Yeats, a Celtic poet whose poetry is magical, where his poetry was, and he said, 'My poetry is here, in the tip of my pen. Before I write anything, there's no poetry. And then the poetry comes out.' It's what some call 'automatic writing'. You don't have to think about it, it just comes out like that.

In my case, I think it's a lot to do with my mother. She was a huge influence on me, and she was very imaginative and poetic; she taught me to trust myself and gave me self-confidence. And then later, I think, she inspired me to write simply because she had very good style and she wrote very, very well. She sent me letters all through my childhood, and so I was being taught – without realising it – how to write well and amusingly.

In terms of the influence of my work, there's a double process that goes on. When you are an academic, unless you're an absolute genius who's changed the whole field, your work very quickly becomes dated. That is to say, new, younger researchers come along and revise the opinions, and the whole subject changes in its direction and the questions it's asking. My students used to complain if I set them books which had been written more than 30 years ago. So, I wouldn't expect young anthropologists, on the whole, unless they were going to Nepal and working, to be reading much of my stuff. One or two books, my *Origins of English Individualism*, possibly, is the book which people still read.

When you retire, your networks of contacts and your influence decline a lot because you don't have students. So, in one way, I'm dead intellectually: Macfarlane, who he? On the other hand, because I've discovered the media and I put up a lot of material on YouTube and did not rely on influential publishers, I'm much more influential than I've ever been because every three or four days I put up a talk or a piece on YouTube and immediately get two or three hundred people watching it, and I get comments and so on.

Thanks to the wonderful work of my colleague and friend Zilan, I have a wide network in China. It is said that a prophet is not known in his own country. That means, if you are in your own place, everyone says, oh, they're unimportant, and if you can transfer to another civilisation or another country, then you have the power of distance and so on, and you could benefit a little bit from that. Thanks to Zilan, I'm probably read by many more people now in China than I ever was and am in Britain. So, forgotten but reborn in your wonderful land – China.

We hope to have one more session together where we will pick up all the questions we've forgotten to ask. But you never know what might happen tomorrow and we might never meet again. There is a saying in Japan when you have a tea ceremony: *ichi-go ichi-e*. It means 'one time, one meeting'. We are here now – friendship, equality, trust, deep meaning. What will happen in the future, we don't know. But for this moment in time, we have communicated as friends.

Timeless Vision ©Tim Yip Studio

Six. 30 May 2023.

Drawing spirit – The second language – Beijing opera. What is and isn't evolution? – Middle East: an opening between East and West – Everyone is Lili – Books and the language of design – Everything is already here – Two things for young people in the West.

AM: So, once again, here we are for another round of our fascinating conversations. Thank you very much for coming.

TY: Thank you.

AM: This one is going to concentrate on your art, with a few other questions. The first one is perhaps very easy to answer: which is your favourite Chinese dynasty? In other words, if you were going to be reborn again, would you want to be in the Song, Southern Song or Northern Song or Han or whatever?

TY: I think Song is the deepest. Art was also very good in Wei Jin Nan Bei Chao[11] around 380. They have created many avant-garde developments in philosophy and art, but the period is terrible because everyone was being killed.

AM: Yes, in a battle.

TY: But the best artists come from there. Also, at the end of the Song dynasty, the culture is remarkably artistic, but it's a bad time in other ways. The Tang dynasty too, I think, is very interesting.

AM: So, if you had to decide, probably Tang is a good combination of stability and creative art. And Buddhism. Interesting Buddhism developments happened then.

TY: Yes. Many things happened. I think the energy was very strong during that dynasty.

AM: The next question is, who are your favourite ancient and contemporary Chinese artists?

TY: Li Bai, a Tang poet. And Gu Kaizhi, a painter.

AM: Why do you like Gu Kaizhi's paintings?

---

11 Wei, Jin and North-South dynasties, a generic term for the period AD 220-589.

TY: Because he draws spirit. His lines establish a kind of aesthetics that belongs to chi. He draws the movement of energy, creating a sense of aliveness on the paper. It's not something physical. It's more like a feeling that lets you experience taste and elegance within yourself. This can't be put into words because it's in everything, in the rhythm, rather than in any specific element. Through his art I learned *qiyun shengdong* (氣韵生動)[12]. This means showing life energy on paper when you draw on it.

AM: Another question about energy: if a child asks you to explain what is rhythm in visual arts, what would you say?

TY: I think colour is rhythm. The interplay of big and small is also rhythm. I think the more interesting rhythm is pattern. How the pattern forms, and how the pattern repeats and reforms, repeats and reforms. This is the rhythm. Almost everything can be translated into patterns. Pattern is like the data of movement. Curved lines express rhythm. Complicated curves express more rhythm.

A complicated rhythm can be shown by softer and wider curves followed by smaller, more abrupt curves, suggesting slow and fast movement. There is a mysterious connection between rhythm and emotion. So, sometimes, when you're seeing abstract visual rhythm, you'll respond to it internally like we respond to music. Music is using this kind of …

AM: I was going to say, rhythm goes across all the arts, doesn't it? Including music. And speech.

TY: And speech, yes. Sometimes when I write, I give it rhythm, to make the reader go into the content.

---

12 A fundamental but complex concept in Chinese aesthetics. Among the attempts to translate it into English are 'rhythmic resonance', 'spirit resonance', 'creating rhythmic vitality', 'spirit resonance and life-motion' and 'spirit consonance engendering a sense of life'.

AM: The next question is: you talked about your favourite ancient Chinese artists – what about contemporary Chinese artists?

TY: Let me see... We don't have many contemporary artists in China. I think we're missing a connection with the ancient, and if we are talking about an incredible Chinese artist, that connection has to be there. Because of conceptual art, the tendency now is to make everything objective; art is no longer from the artist himself, it's not from his eyes focussing on critical points to make something different. But I would love to be able to connect with a rhythm of tradition and create modern contemporary art in that way. I think this will be very interesting.

AM: Is anyone else doing that in China?

TY: There are a few. For example, I have worked with Ang Lee, who is not a contemporary artist, but he's doing something like what I'm describing. I have difficulty saying that I am a contemporary artist because it seems that contemporary artists are more conceptual and not usually aware of or related to the past, and for me this feels very strange. Conceptual art was here already from the 60s.

AM: Really? As early as that?

TY: Yes. Before that, I think, art was more related to Impressionism. Then Post-Impressionism. Then came Duchamp with the urinal. He started conceptual art. He said that everything put in the museum will be art. And if I put my name on it, it will be art. Everything started from there. Maybe it had meaning at the time, but later on it became something like tricks, and it broke the connection with all the origins. I want to get back the connection with the ancient. When you get back that connection, there will no longer be fragmented energy. When concepts are imposed and declared to be right, then everything is silent. But when the richness and diversity of perception comes out, everything can give and share energy. Contemporary art as I practise it means going in that direction.

I have a big question. Now is a very special time. The meaning of being human has been constructed for a long time by cultures of the world. Afterwards this was taken over by a concept, and after that is became a system. We are living in the system now because the system is helping us to get everything together, at least physically. But now artificial intelligence and other developments are coming, and human beings don't even have a clear property. It's as if the human identity is fading away. Of course, some will say that humans are being replaced by machines, but that's an extreme view. I think now is the time to think about what was before, what humans believed themselves to be in the world and what has been taken away from that. What do you think about the loss of human identity?

AM: Well, interestingly, I went to a talk since we met last by someone who was at my college, a man called Geoffrey Hinton. He's known as the godfather of artificial intelligence. And he's just left Google because he's worried about the direction AI is taking. He was asked what his two main existential worries were.

He said the small one was that Donald Trump would become elected president again, aided by artificial intelligence and social media as he was last time. Hinton has left America and gone to Toronto, Canada.

His longer-term existential worry is what some people call 'the singularity', when computers become more intelligent than human beings. He and most people thought this would be about 35 years from now, but he now says his guess is somewhere between 5 and 15 years. Maybe even 2 years. I mean, it could be. And he put it in the way that you've mentioned, which is that maybe evolution meant that different species occur and dominate the world, and the biological organisms which you and I are had a long period, and we have now evolved or will be evolving into a digital machine sphere.

I tried to argue with him in just two minutes afterwards (and he's coming back, I hope, to do an interview with me next year). I put it to him that such a view suggests that human beings will just become the pets of machines. Machines will be much cleverer and so on. But I was thinking about all previous technological breakthroughs in human history, and the thing about machines is that we have developed them as extensions of ourselves, which for a time do particular jobs extremely well. The first great revolution was from the Palaeolithic to the Neolithic. We domesticated animals and made them our servants. Then in the industrial revolution we made machines which could do things for us. And so, the AI revolution is yet another time when we develop machines which we can use to do specific jobs. Now, they talk about general AI, though at the moment it's specific things it does extremely well.

He suggested – and this is what I argue with – that these machines will be able to understand or know everything human beings can know by language. He suggested that if you put a baby in a room like this with just a radio and no other human beings, and the radio played natural language all the time, then after some months or years this child would be a normal thinking human being. I said to him this is nonsense because there have been many cases of babies who have been shut off from other human beings and lived with animals or whatever, and they've been mentally very disturbed.

I referred to one of the great theories of how the human mind works, David Hume's *Enquiry Concerning Human Understanding*. Hume's theory, as you know, is that all we understand about the world is from experience and from sensations. We only learn about the world through our five senses, from our eyes, ears, smell, touch and so on. Until machines can do that – until they can travel around, see, smell, hear and then process it in a way similar to a biological neural network – until that time comes, which may or may not happen, they will be different from us. They will be just processing patterns and not understanding anything. He just smiled and said David Hume was wrong. We'll have to see.

Coming back to your question, I think artificial intelligence and other things like that are making us reassess what it is to be human beings. That happens quite often in human history when there are big ruptures. An obvious example in our Western history is the Renaissance because the great painters, artists and writers of the Renaissance, anyone from Leonardo to William Shakespeare, were faced with new things which were intruding on their world. It made them reassess who they were as human beings. Another period was in the late 19th century with the birth of the social sciences, like my discipline, anthropology. We in the West thought we knew what human beings were, and then suddenly all these alternatives, possibilities and combinations which we'd never thought of began to be presented from discovering worlds which were based on totally different principles. So, you had to hugely expand your idea of what a human being was to encompass everyone from the simplest to the most complex, to new civilisations. So, there had been periods when we were doing that.

Having lived through the computer revolution in Cambridge, up till quite recently it didn't make you do that. It made you aware of the Internet and how powerful computers were, but artificial intelligence suddenly makes you think, well, what is it that's distinctive about humanity and differentiates it from any other thing? We're just doing that. For many people it is threatening and causes anxiety, worry and so on. But also, it's enormously stimulating and makes one really grow, look into oneself and understand. I'm finding it both those things. I'm not very anxious because I'm old, and I'll be gone by the time these machines come. But it is extremely stimulating.

And to end, it's a double stimulation because this whole artificial intelligence situation is making me wonder what my world is and who I am, but likewise the rise of China. Zilan and I went to see a very interesting Chinese artist last week. He's a calligrapher, Wang Dongling. Do you know of him?

TY: Yes, I have heard about him.

AM: He's a professor of calligraphy at Hangzhou Academy of Arts. A really nice man, very interesting. We had dinner with him, and I met him twice and watched him painting. Hearing him talk I suddenly realised that Chinese civilisation and the things you're interested in going back to are so different in every respect from my world. The deeper I go into it, the more it makes me question my own world.

So, artificial intelligence and China make me think about my own world. Anyway, I talked for quite a long time there, so let me ask you another question. Quite a simple one. You've referred once or twice to your enthusiasm and liking of Beijing opera, and some of your art has mirrors or reflections of Beijing opera. Why do you like Beijing opera so much?

TY: In Chinese literature there is *fu bi xing* (賦比興). The three ways of expression in literature. The middle part, *bi*, is putting two places or situation side by side to hint at the similarity and the mutual mirroring of two worlds. They let different worlds coexist.

When Mei Lanfang dressed as a woman and performed his 'orchid gestures' with his hands and fingers, these became formula. But when you see it, you feel a very special thing is happening. It's like a second language, the language of suggestion. It speaks of something real but not talked about in ordinary language in the physical world. It's something like poetic language, though it's more than that. It speaks of something already there. Maybe a man has a woman's emotions and tendencies within, but after passing through the door of time and space he becomes a man. But everything that was within him is still there. Making these gestures would collect all these veiled tendencies and emotions and turn them into a formula. Or, for example, long sleeves could be suggestive of strong emotions and act as an extension of the actor's movements, especially in Beijing opera.

I find the coexistence of this kind of translation or extension with ordinary performance very powerful. Mythologies talk in these ways, and I can relate to many things there. The famous Chinese ghost stories are really about the human world, but at that time it wasn't possible to speak directly, so they had to be written as ghost stories. Li Bai has a poem where he uses such mirroring to talk about the heaven he's never been to. But for me this second language isn't just fancy. What it expresses is real. It hasn't come from nowhere. But you can't use normal words to talk about this. You can talk about flying to hint at the lightness of energy. And when you understand the lightness of energy, you understand calligraphy, the control of rhythm on the paper. Everything you draw on the paper will affect the whole future of the paper because of the pull towards balance. I feel this language gives me a way of seeing the complicated world.

Jingju (京劇),[13] I think, goes back a very long time as popular entertainment for a mass audience. You see, Beijing opera has several dimensions. One of them is court dance. It's slow and entertaining in a way. But another dimension of Jingju is street performance. There was very little light, maybe a bit from a fire, so the performers had to have something glittering on their costumes. This way people standing far away in the audience could see the performance. The glittering costumes are not something deliberately designed. It's a way to share energy with all of the audience. Then it became a standard feature of Jingju costumes. When the performers needed to convey a character's tragic inner state, they added the long sleeves which mirrored and magnified the performer's arm movements and transmitted the emotion to those watching the performance from far away.

AM: Did you get the long sleeves in your films from Beijing opera?

TY: Yes. And the flags on a character's back. Flags indicate a military commander with troops following him. He uses the flags to direct different parts of his army.

---

13 Beijing opera.

Beijing opera performers are different from Western ones. In the West, a dancer just dances, and a singer just sings. But in Beijing opera one person should be able to do many different things. They have no sets and no stage props. All they have is basic acting props, for example a horse would be just a stick. Everything becomes symbolic. The performers have to communicate in an evocative way. For example, when you want to show that you are going through a doorway, you have to lift you legs as if stepping over an invisible bar, because all doors had a bar at the bottom. It seems as if they are acting in an invisible world. I learned a lot from that.

AM: There is a follow-up question. I have only been to Beijing opera once or twice, but I was interested in Japanese theatre. They have two: Kabuki and Noh. Kabuki is Osaka; it's merchants, it's humorous, it's down to earth. Women, *onnagata* and so on. Noh, the other form, is very strange. It's all dark. And a lot of ghosts. It's a very ancient form of shamanic memories kept into the present, so it's basically shamans performing various rituals. I was wondering to what extent Beijing opera is supernatural. You mentioned invisible things, but are there elements in it also which are about ancient Daoist or other beliefs?

TY: Yes. In general, you can say that Beijing opera is different in the north and in the south. The northern version is faster, and the singing is rougher. The sound is rougher. The southern version is slower, more beautiful.

AM: When you say south, is it in Beijing or in the south of China?

TY: Jiangnan. It's in Hangzhou, Suzhou.

AM: Really? There's a Beijing opera there?

TY: Yes. And it's different.

AM: So, it's closer to Kunqu.

TY: Exactly. There are two influences. One is court dance. It's like Noh – slow, beautiful dancing in a big hall. The other is like Kung Fu: *za shua* (杂耍), acrobatics – acrobatic performances in festivals and things like that. Kunqu doesn't have the acrobatic part. The beginning of Kunqu is people getting together and singing in a setting similar to court dance. There are no big sets or props. But Jingju is something similar to mass entertainment. There is a mix of fighting, jokes, comedy, acrobatics. The purpose was to amaze and entertain the people. There were also special features that came into Jingju from local theatre, I think. All this was developed and combined into a language. This makes Jingju special for me. I can see that it was constantly moving and evolving. In the mid-Qing dynasty it was totally different from what we think of as Beijing opera now. It kept changing and changed a lot. But it stopped in the 1930s, I think.

AM: It hasn't been revived? You said it stopped in the 1930s.

TY: It became completely different. Now it has more modern technologies, more video projections.The dancing, I think, had a lot of influence from Western modern dance. The traditional side is sort of there too. For example, good friends of mine in Taiwan set up the Contemporary Legend Theatre. They are using Jingju to stage Greek tragedies and Shakespeare. *Macbeth*, for example. They do it in Chinese costume and through Chinese-style performance. Also, Richard Schechner, the American director, came and we worked together to make a show in a garden, so it became environmental theatre. You could say Beijing opera evolved, but I understand evolution in a different way. I think the evolution of Jingju stopped with Mei Lanfang. His innovations were in the traditional spirit. There was continuity. After that the modern came in. And the modern influences aren't recent, I think. Mei Lanfang went to Shanghai in 1912, and Feng Zihe, another famous actor, was working there on incorporating certain Western influences into Jingju, adding a stage-like setup, since there was a lot of Western influence in Shanghai in general. They started having paintings as part of this stage setup, for example there would be a garden painting and small furniture of similar theme, sort of like props supporting a story in drama. The traditional setup was just a table and two chairs. It was the same everywhere. And a red curtain behind. Actors had to do everything themselves. You had to guess. The presence of painting brought in other layers. This is already on the edge of my definition of evolution. I believe evolution should develop organically from the tradition. Now the modern elements are just put in from outside. They are not connected with anything within the tradition.

I had a chance to do a big show in Suzhou, many years ago. I worked with a scholar who was also a director. We talked in depth and researched the traditional appearance of the characters. They were totally different. The appearances were changed by individual actors. There were no fixed rules, and the actor could change pretty much anything. When an actor is successful, his interpretation of the appearance becomes the new standard. For example, before Mei Lanfang, the hairline was straight. But Mei Lanfang brought in the distinctive hairline with seven waves, and everyone started doing that afterwards. But still, they came from the form of the total art. The organic whole of how the acting, singing and dancing came together remained. It's different from abruptly deciding to make a stage just because you want to make a stage. In my opinion, we can do it abstractly in the Chinese way. It's not a physical thing like drama. This to me is not evolution. When there are such sudden insertions, the art form itself changes. It's not the same.

I'd love to ask you... I am acutely aware that the world is changing very fast. But usually, things change from a base. Now it's not like that.

AM: It's something suspended.

TY: Yes. And unknown. The only known is the multi-effects. Technology is becoming so powerful that everything can be changed. Before, when we wanted to change something, we had to move the base. Now we don't have to move the base. Everything can change every second. The effect is, we have become reactive. Young people can't react from direct experience, because they were born into a world of facts and data. They are always looking something up on the Internet. They know many things, but they know them from the Internet, not by experiencing them through touch and other senses. No life. Just data and knowledge.

You have studied the past and know how things were. And you see what is happening now. You can see both sides. Now is a good time to think: we are at the very gates of the artificial intelligence period. How do you feel about the young generation when you talk to them? Are they different?

AM: I remember being in China some years ago with a young friend at university. She was 22, I suppose, or 21, and she said, 'I don't understand people two years younger than me at university. China is changing so fast that even two years is a huge gap in knowledge.' I think most older people in this country feel that. I was talking about this with my daughter yesterday, and she said she can roughly understand me, and I can roughly understand her, though there is a big gap. But the next generation, in other words my grandchildren, I find I don't understand them, and they don't understand me. I can see that when I'm with them they're not with me, they're distracted by their phones, what they're watching and so on. Their attention is not really on me at all, and I can't talk to them at a meaningful level. That's the depressing, kind of sad thing.

On the other hand, when I meet young people seriously, in a context like Cambridge, when I meet schoolchildren wanting to come to Cambridge or undergraduates of Cambridge, I feel it's very easy to talk to them, to communicate, and we seem to understand each other perfectly well. I can teach them perfectly well. So, if the context is right, there is really no difference. A lot of the references I'll mention – people, places, books – they've never heard of them, and vice versa. The content of their cultural world and knowledge world is very different from mine. And yet when we get down to discussing things, then quite often it's very easy to have a genuinely interesting conversation with them. I don't feel that their minds have changed or that they are different human beings, I just feel that they are being bombarded with all sorts of data which aren't like mine. One of the big questions in anthropology was, if you go to a remote tribe in Africa or New Guinea or Amazonia, or even if you go to China or Japan, will you be able to understand the other person because their life's experience, their whole way of thinking, their cosmology, their logic, their upbringing are so different from yours that maybe there'll be no possibility. In fact, David Hume says that, however clever you are, if you meet something you've never encountered before, then you won't be able to understand it. My encouraging experience is that wherever I go in the world, as long as we can share some language or I can talk through someone, it's very easy. In other words, it confirms the anthropological belief that human beings are alike, that the differences are very small, that the similarity is very great, and that as soon as I begin to spend time in any part of the world I can start to make jokes, and they laugh, and we can talk about deep things easily with people who are either literate or uneducated, men or women, children or grown-ups, so that I find it very easy to communicate. That being the case with civilisations and societies so different from my own, it shouldn't be very difficult to communicate with young people, as long as you can get their attention. So, the world is spinning as if it's out of control, but actually human beings are very capable of pulling it together and understanding each other.

TY: That's wonderful.

I know that you are developing the academic library project and that you have already written many beautiful books about your work and experiences. What is it that you haven't started yet but want to accomplish?

AM: This reminds me of Donald Rumsfeld. What are the unknown unknowns? If I haven't started it, I won't know what it is.

One thought I've had recently is, I'm finishing off eight books at the moment, and what is the one beyond that? Well, one I may have mentioned before is I've approached my autobiography through writing it as an autobiography, through analysing it, but there are three further ways of looking at it. One is through my library. This was suggested by my wife. We're going to look at how a library is constructed. How we bought the books, why we bought the books, what the books mean to us, what a library is. This is partly because libraries are disappearing, though you have a very big one, and I hope to show you mine this afternoon which is smaller. But the extension of the human mind into the age of the book is something which I'd like to record because, my wife being a bookseller and I a collector of books and an academic having quite a big library, we could probably make a very nice book about what an academic's library is. So, that's one.

The same with our garden and the house because our garden has evolved with us and is an outside, outward projection. My form of art is basically our garden, our house, our objects in it and so on. That would be a documentation because we've got lots of film, we've got photographs, and we've got our diaries, so you can see how a human being makes and constructs a world around them in a garden, and it connects with gardens in China, Japan and so on. The world of the garden and the mind of the garden and magic gardens is another one.

The last thing is related to what I've mentioned before, that I felt as if I'm climbing up a mountain and can see the world better and better. But I realised at times that maybe I'm near the top of a mountain, or over the top, and there is a danger, and this is why I'm fortunate to have my wife and good friends like Zilan who will say, 'don't go on with that, don't do that because it isn't you at your best: you are either declining or you're going in a direction which you shouldn't go in.' Just yesterday I wrote a piece about why I'm so despairing about America and how it's wasted its opportunity; it could have made this world wonderful, and it's just wasted it. I came across the statistic that the Americans spent 3 trillion dollars on the military in Afghanistan, and they spent 3 billion dollars on aid and development. If the Americans had spent half of their huge budget on development aid, and only half on military support, Afghanistan would be one of the richest, happiest countries in the world. Or if they'd spent it on water, the whole world would have proper water supplies. It's a great tragedy that they wasted on war what they could have spent on peace. I sent it to a friend, and she said, 'Alan, this isn't you at your best. You're not usually so negative and aggressive. Let's put it on one side, think about it and maybe improve it or do something like that.'

At my stage, though compared to some people I'm still quite young, there is a danger, and it's a particular danger now, I think, because it's so much easier to write. Before I had to sit and write a draft, and then I'd type it, and then I'd rewrite it – that slows you down. Now I can just talk into a computer, AI transforms it into text, and it's ready to be published. So, there is some danger that I make things too simple because what happens as you get older is that the world seems to get simpler and simpler, and so I shock people by saying that China is very simple to understand and that all you need is these six things. I may be right, but maybe I've oversimplified China a bit. So, a mixture of arrogance, age and ease of communication means that I have to be careful in what I write next.

TY: That is very good.

AM: Let's just have one more round of questions. You've been to a lot of countries, and you started going to Continental countries and others when you were young. Which country or which culture have you not been to and you would like to visit, and why?

TY: Saudi Arabia, I think. I am a book collector, and books published in the past 100 years, even internationally, are influenced by the West. But Arabia is not easy to get into very closely because they closed the door. It's an unknown place, even the Muslim culture, the beautiful patterns, buildings and other things. We don't understand it because it's not very common. But now, in the past 10-20 years, they opened, and places like Dubai welcome international artists to come and create there. It's possible that many things came from the Arab world. For example, China always says that everything came from the land. But it's a symbolic area. There are Mongolian scholars who say that even things we think of as very Chinese, like dragons, may have come from outside China. And horses too.

AM: Yes. They came from Central Asia.

TY: I also think that the Middle East was maybe the beginning of the East-West division, and that makes me very interested. There is wide use of patterns and all kinds of original things there. I started listening to the music. In the Arab culture some say that music is not right and it's wrong to listen to music. So, you have to be silent. You can't just sing. And there is also the women's clothing. It seems there are many ways to protect women from being too much in the world.

AM: The music thing is complicated. It's like a lot of art in certain branches of Islam. As you know, in the Middle East you have to distinguish the different branches of Islam like Sunni, Shi'a. It's only some branches which are anti-music and anti-representational art. I tried to understand that area, and it's very difficult for me too. But if you look at the three banned things – drinking alcohol, representational art and music – all of them are joined together by one thing, which is that they are too powerful. They distract the mind from God. And so, the objection to them is the same as Plato's objection to poetry and painting. He said that they take over your emotions and divert them, and therefore you can no longer think clearly. It was the same thing with extreme forms of religion and Calvinism in this country, which disapproved of many of the arts because they said they play too much to the senses and the emotional side of you and take away from your devotion and your rational self and relation to God. What you said is very interesting because I think that is going to be a big development, the opening up of the Middle East, because for a long time it's been under huge pressure from outside, particularly from America, and from being involved in wars between various groups. Now, with the agreement the Chinese brokered between Iran and Saudi Arabia and with opening up of Syria, the Middle East is relaxing. It's detaching itself from the West. Not attaching itself necessarily to China, but it's becoming more confident and separate. And a place where all sorts of experiments are beginning to take place in all sorts of fields, and it would be very exciting if someone like you went there.

TY: I find that they are really welcoming, and we have to open our eyes to see clearly what is happening. As you said, this detaching happened, and the changing of the whole world, and suddenly they opened up. I believe that we should look carefully, so we can see the truth.

AM: One last question before lunch. Let's have a question about dear Lili here. You mentioned that you are making specialised Lilis. But just as *Dao De Jing* says that 'three gives rise to ten thousand things', will the world of Lilis become just as complex as the ordinary reality, the play of yin and yang constantly harmonising?

TY: I think you can say that it has happened. Everyone is Lili. That's also the concept. She does not exist. She is a reflection. I just put her in the area of the known and unknown periods, the reflection of the human. Even for things that will happen in the future I can use her now, to let the people understand what the future is. That is the idea. Why can she evolve into different forms? Because she does not exist. She is just a reflection. When you come up the street you can see a reflection on the water – that is Lili. You see in the window there is wind in the curtains making them move – this is Lili. It's a magic power because she does not exist, but she is physically present. You have a familiar thing, and you want to fill it up. It's like a black hole in a way. When you see wine, you feel it's wine. When you feel Lili is there, it's a reflection of what you experience.

She can change to another dimension. That's what I'm developing. My next exhibition will be devoted to the many different possibilities of Lili. There will be something like natural Lili, reflecting the possibility where humans are destroyed and have to get back to their origin and start again as species alongside plants and other life forms, and change their DNA to become part of nature. Because of her I can think of something like that. She is just sitting beside you today, in 2023. But she can also become an infinity figure. It's like she opens the limitation of time and space for us. But she is physical, and you can feel her co-exist with you. This is one of the things that I feel is very interesting about this work. Also, people react to her. There are so many things to find out.

AM: Just a comment, so it's not really relevant. One of my favourite writers is Jorge Luis Borges, and in one of his short stories, called *Tlön, Uqbar, Orbis Tertius*, a man discovers one volume of an encylopaedia describing another world. He reads it. Then he accidentally obtains another volume. And then gradually this world is taken over by the encylopaedia of the other world. The things in the other world begin to inhabit this world and destroy it in the end. I hope Lili will not destroy our world by peopling it, however lovely she is. I hope there will be room for a few human beings as well. Anyway… Lili, time for lunch!

*

AM: We're coming to our last session, for the moment anyway. You're an incredibly creative, versatile artist, and I wondered, what are the main sources of your creativity? It's always many different things, but is it books? Is it dreams? Is it experiences? Is it travel? Is it conversations? If you had to put them in an order of importance, how would you arrange them?

TY: When I was a child, I was very shy, and I could never get what I wanted because I didn't know how to ask. I have an elder brother, and he always got everything I wanted because he's really strong and articulate, and people paid attention to him. I always felt I was second best. That went on for a long time, and when I was working with a director doing art direction, I would go on working even when the director wasn't very good. But as time went on, I noticed that when I did what I wanted, the result was always better. So, I started trying to do it myself. But of course, when you are doing something yourself, it is very difficult to get it to be as good as you want. I always have this kind of curiosity, and I want to be better than other people.

I didn't get into university when I was young, and…

AM: Did you try?

TY: Yes, but not very hard. At that time people who came out of the Chinese University and Hong Kong University were considered to be on a higher level. So, I wanted to be a university student, but it never happened. But I think I'm not well suited to being at school. My study has to be about something I really want, and I will use my full energy to find it. I'm not well suited to waiting and going very slowly, as they do at school. Or maybe the school was not very good in Hong Kong.

In any case, I always studied on my own to compete with all these university students, and it became my habit. I always wanted to learn something that would make me better than others because they might have heard something in lectures, but I developed it from within.

So, as I mentioned earlier, I started creating a map of people, times and places. There I collected everything I liked. Photographs. Renaissance paintings. With each entry, I would keep notes on why I liked the piece. I had thousands of entries, including classical music, modern music, anything. From these I created a book of my sensory perceptions which became for me a way of looking at the world. But this practice made my ego even bigger, and I wanted to know even more.

When I understood a topic, I would think of another angle of looking at it. I studied from books and had many books of my own. I would want to know something, so I'd buy a book about it and read the book. Then I'd read the work of people who held different views on this topic and approached it from different angles. I found I didn't believe anything I saw, but I made a note of the possibilities I came across, without fixing anything firmly. And I noted possible ways of growth and interconnections with other things. So, I always had a kind of invisible mandala in front of me. If I found a gap in it, I would buy books, research the topic and fill the gap.

Reading books so much made me pay attention to the books themselves. I started noticing details like who designed the book, what was the author's influence, how they looked at things, how they chose the pictures for the book.

And slowly, I found that from the 70s onwards, people really concentrated on design. The design became a language. And when the author sees this book, they will feel, oh this is good. You find that when you look within his book, there's a lot of influence from the cover, or the feel of the book. These details can make you feel more. So, the book is like a curation. The knowledge is just knowledge. Now in digital times knowledge is turned into data, and data gives you the answer. Really simple. But when you're reading a book, it's like somebody already curated the material and then gave it to you. It's different. I believe in that kind of grey area to make you get more feeling about things. Sometimes publishers, like Taschen, produce their books in a standardised format, but if the book is really designed, the effect will be different.

I remember in the 80s they started to have books that seemed to have a life of their own. They would talk about things but without using words. These were specially designed books. They spoke the language of design, not the language of words. This always makes me feel that we are in an invisible world at the same time. Words are created for human beings to communicate, but that kind of thing is another layer to deepen the content.

This helped me look at movies in a new way. When I worked with Ang Lee, I understood that it's not just one scene. It's not like I'm talking about something big, and then I have to make every scene big. It's about creating a motion, a development. The whole movie is a development to that high point. Everything is prepared. The audience follows this development because of the preparation. We always see the underlying curve. That's really important.

Later I saw this in other areas of life. In photography, for example. Something suddenly comes to your intuition, and you have to take the photograph in a certain way. Any photographer, any artist in general has this sort of sensitivity. When a sculptor sees a material, it's like *boom*, and he feels a shape coming up strongly. And then he really knows how to finish the piece. When we look at the sculpture in the museum, we would find its beginning, what gave that initial impetus for the shape to form. Rhythm is derived from emotion. It's something abstract, actually, but very close to the human mind, though it's not thinking. It's more like a feeling, and a force that gives rise to a strongly formed shape. It's the expression. The expression, or… you need something to get away from you. Every time you create, you want to take away something. It's so hard. You have to use all your power to let it out into the work. Afterwards, when you see it in the work, you feel release. Then you see clearly, and you are reborn. Every time you create something fully, fully satisfying, you will be reborn. You have a chance to be reborn, to get new energy, new space. You've freed space up by releasing the previous work. It's already finished. It doesn't belong to me. I can focus on other things.

That's why when I finish a movie and it's really satisfying, I don't immediately start the next one. Instead, I do theatre or something else. I want to put myself into a place which I'm not used to, where I don't have a habit. I want to keep the distance and feel the energy, feel the misunderstanding. There are so many different interesting things. It's unlimited, I think. I don't believe in answers. I believe in exploring.

When you close your eyes and open them, you see the world again. It's all there. It's just how much you see. It's not you who creates it. It's already there. I just have to find it. I'm not in a hurry because everything is there. It's not about my creating it or not. It's how much I can see. So, I don't want to fix the direction of what I want to find. I suddenly have an emotion, and I see something. So, everything is focussed on different parts. It totally belongs to the sensations. That sensation is very important. The sensation will drive your emotion to action. Maybe you smell something, and you want to eat. Maybe you see something beautiful, and you want to touch it. Some music is really going into your mind, and you want to listen to it more. That kind of very simple reaction.

Everything is already there. I just pick what I need. Sometimes I would ask somebody for help. For example, if I'm going to a forest and don't know much about forests, I'd ask an expert for help. I don't have to do everything myself. I just ask for help. It happens very naturally, and I do it more and more often. I feel I can do anything because when I don't know how to do something, I can ask somebody else to do it. But I know when to start the piece and when to stop. Technical experts may not know it, but I do. I have an inner feeling of how to direct the whole thing.

I am interested in everything. But also, we could say that times are not very peaceful now. Now is the time when there is a lot to do. When you meditate, you find the balance. But sometimes the balance can't be found. So, everything will come up to action and creation to find the balance again. I meet many different people who feel the same way. It's interesting how people with a creative mind open wider and wider and get together to form a balance.

AM: That's a very interesting answer. Thank you.

TY: I often think about and re-read Goethe's Faust, and I wonder, if an angel came to you and offered you a chance to start again, which period of time or which world would you choose to go to?

AM: Maybe more than one…

The first is a joke really: the Garden of Eden, as in some of those wonderful Renaissance paintings that I like, Savery and others. I would like to be in the Garden of Eden because then you have no pain, no suffering, everything is easier and so on. And I would like to be there so that I could change history because when God came and saw these innocent happy human beings and said 'everything is fine but don't eat that apple,' I would have liked to have taken God on one side and said, look, if you don't want them to eat that apple, why put it there? And in any case, if you want them to be innocent and happy, leave it like that. But if you're encouraging, or if you create a creature, a snake, which is there tempting them, why do you do that? Why destroy what you've made? So, I would like to have a conversation with God and persuade Him that He was going to make a number of mistakes. And if He said, no, no, they must learn the knowledge of what is good and what is evil, I would have said what I think often about Milton's portrayal of the Garden of Eden and the fall of man, that what God was really frightened of was that when they ate the apple and learned about good and evil, they would realise that there is no difference. God wanted them to say, this is good, that is evil. But in Chinese thought, in Daoism and many philosophical systems, good and evil are like yin and yang. They are not separate, and there is always good in evil and evil in good. And so, the whole binary downfall of Satan in Milton's poem isn't recognised in most philosophies. There is no absolute good or evil in Buddhism either. I would have tried to persuade God that it was both foolish of Him and also mistaken to try and create binaries. That's one time I would have gone back to.

Another time and place… there are so many… I would have loved to have been in Italy in the 15th century, particularly with Leonardo and some of the great artists, watching them and learning about them.

Another one – and again a joke – I would have liked to have been in England in the late 16th century, Queen Elizabeth's time, and to have tried to find out who was writing Shakespeare's plays. Because these plays are so extraordinary, their deep understanding of human nature and posing of many of the deepest problems that we face. What kind of person could have written those plays? The conventional view, as you know, is that it was quite a humble person living in a small English town, Stratford-on-Avon, who went to a small English school. And yet, although I have great confidence that anyone can do anything, I struggle with the thought that someone from that background could have understood world history and philosophy and different countries so well and then written these fantastic plays, and yet not left a single trace of himself – there is no actual fact linking the William Shakespeare of Stratford-on-Avon to the plays, you know; they're side by side. So, I would have loved to have been there and done some detective work to find out who it really was. It might have been him; it might have been someone else.

Finally, I would like to have been here at the year 2023, in a room in Cambridge, and have had the extraordinary opportunity to meet a great artist who lives in invisible worlds, takes me back into ancient China and opens up new doors to my understanding.

The first three wishes may not be granted, but the fourth has been granted in meeting you, Tim. So, that's my answer.

One more question for you. You are trying to bring to the West your deeper understandings of ancient Chinese philosophy and art, and China in general. If you had a young person, shall we say Lili, an English Lili, and you had a few things that they really needed to think about and understand in order to understand your Eastern world, what would you tell them?

TY: I think the first thing would be about freedom. When I did the first *Love Infinity*, I found that everyone was crying for freedom and self-expression. But I noticed that they are all very lonely. If you take freedom as a concept, you will be alone in the end, because no one can share it with you, since you want to be free every minute. It's a tricky thing in social education, I think. These artists were always thinking and talking about 'doing it myself'. But what is the meaning of doing it yourself? It is something misunderstood. They become easy prey for capitalists who offer them money. The artist might think, I am doing it myself because I have funding. But in the end, the funding directs you to a wrong place – you are not really doing it yourself.

These things are complicated, but I found some answers from one of the interviewees who said, oh, I don't think it's really interesting to be sitting on the beach and talking about something like global warming. To some people freedom is when I am enjoying what I want to do, I am enjoying what I express, but I am not enjoying giving. But real freedom is about responding.

When I have something, I will think about who is missing this thing, because I have it already. Freedom is when I don't eat it because I want everyone else to eat it. This is really difficult, but in ancient times the Chinese talked about *rang* (让). It means a particular form of giving: I don't take it because when I don't take it, everyone can take it; if I take it, only I can take it. They have this kind of philosophy.

And there is a famous Chinese story about people sitting around the table, and everyone has very long chopsticks. You take some food with your chopsticks, but you can't eat it because your chopsticks are too long. So, what to do so that everyone around the table can eat? You give the food to each other. That's totally right because everyone can eat, but you take it from somebody who gives. It is really important to understand what is *xu shi* (虚实). Yin-yang. How to give, how to get. When you say 'get', you are also thinking about 'give'. It's the same word. But in a rational world, I give to you, and you make a deal. It becomes a different thing. When you share things, it becomes endless. I just give to you, and you will receive and return. That is connection. But rationally, when I give to you, you have to give back. When you do not give back, we are separated. We become enemies. It's complicated to explain this. It's the way to get yourself to be free, but at the same time you have to give. You have to discipline yourself, but you can get free. Really free. Free to give.

AM: That's actually one of the many sayings of Jesus. To be free you have to serve others or be responsible towards others. Freedom is service rather than having things. It's giving things. It's in a lot of philosophies. In anthropology there is a lot of discussion about the gift. The gift is something which can either, as you say, be detached – you can give something and then wait, and then they give something back or they don't give back. Or it can be a relationship in which in the giving you are also receiving. In fact, Jesus also said it's better to give than to receive. This is something which most people, if they are lucky, discover, that what causes us most fulfilment, happiness and freedom is giving to other people. There is no greater happiness than giving something of your own and it being received with happiness by someone else. That's much more than just appropriating it.

TY: There is an even deeper thing about which I would have told the young people, that can be communicated with spiritual DNA. When we speak of emptiness, we are speaking of things that speech cannot communicate, and it all seems far away and unreal. But spiritual DNA offers another way that is closer to ordinary thinking. We could say, here is wine, and talk about who makes the wine and who drinks it, and then say that we're not just talking about the bottle. This example can be extended to other contexts.

When you were jokingly talking about going back to the Garden of Eden and arguing with God about the story with the apple, I kept thinking that people did not make a mistake. Every single time we think, we are eating that apple again, and therefore committing that same old mistake again. It seems like this story is about the need for trust, for a relationship without questions. You have the full feeling of the invisible power, and you are in a state of full devotion. Something like that. Everyone who does that will go in the right direction. But we find that difficult because the Devil comes along to make everyone crazy. We can't stay in the state of silent trust and have to deal with internal chaos and desires.

In ancient philosophy they inhabited not just the material world but also what's beyond it. They were bettering themselves, like in Daoism, and practising to have good access to this invisible world. For such people it's not about the benefit of the material as such, but using the material, using your body to feel the infinite, using drugs or other things to make your energy become pure and get back to the infinite. This is totally different. It's not like a mathematical manipulation. It's a living, breathing thing, so that we can all share together by giving.

Nowadays, when we don't have enough material things, we feel sad or lost. People are busy operating with logic and concepts. Even in the family, when you overhear an argument between a couple, it would usually be about material things. The meaning of equality is just as material. So, at the end, they can give or be given to in the rational way I've just talked about. This separates people.

Before you had family to support you. Now everyone is trying to become an individual. Older people have nobody to take care of them because everyone wants to be an individual. But if everyone is like that, then you have to fight for living. There is no other choice and this can make you change your moral point of view. It's a different quality of thought that makes people like that, using concepts for everything, and having everything arranged in separate boxes, so that if I need to make a decision, I can get these boxes out and neatly solve the problem. Overreliance on concepts leads to communication turning into an exercise in cleverness. It's not a real conversation anymore. Everyone knows how to manipulate words and logic and turn things into something else for their own benefit. But we all know why the word was important in the beginning. Because the word was with the moral power then, as the Bible says. Word has moral power when everyone goes into an idealistic world with this word. But now this word has become right or wrong. And based on benefit. It's something different. I think this is quite complicated because we are in the middle of it, and it's difficult to see it. It's all mixed together.

I wonder what you expect for the future. We know what happened in the past. But what is the best version of the future?

AM: Often when people are asked this, they talk about what they hope for the future rather than what they expect.

TY: I'm not asking about hope. I mean things you see unfolding.

AM: Well, I think we talked about this before. The first thing to say is that whatever I say is wrong. Second is that it's going to be very inaccurate because things can happen tomorrow, which means that if you ask me this question tomorrow, for example, some war might have broken out or they discovered there was a new epidemic or something, then my answer will be different. So, each day one's answer is different.

But at the moment, if I'm feeling cheerful, and it depends on whether you mean the future in five years, ten years, a hundred years, but supposing it's the future over the next generation, I expect and hope that the world will become more peaceful and that the realignment of the world so that the West is not so dominant means that a Western point of view which is very competitive, aggressive, scientific and expansive, will be balanced by a point of view from the rest of the world, India, China and so on. And that will adjust decision making, so that instead of wasting most of our resources on weapons and war we will learn to use these resources to deal with the huge problems of global warming and everything else.

If we share what we have and we use the very rapidly growing power of technologies which will potentially give us limitless energy, limitless non-animal foods, cures for most diseases including old age, dementia and so on, then we could actually return to a world where most people could lead a decent, satisfying, creative life. They could spend their time much as a successful Chinese Mandarin did, painting, calligraphy, art, poetry, leisure, friendship, family. There's no reason why eight billion people on this planet couldn't live in that reasonable way given the resources and knowledge that are already available. It just needs a readjusting of our priorities, so that we behave collectively in the interests of the world, rather than our narrow national or group self-interest.

It's never happened up till now. Expecting it to happen now is perhaps a little hopeful, but sometimes one feels that hope lies in young people because quite a lot of the young people I meet are becoming wiser. They're not just spending their time on their phone. They're doing lots of creative things. They're exploring the world. They're interested in and they're trying to do things like improving the climate. So, if the younger generation, as I've seen it in China and to a certain extent over here, persuade older generations to stop this stupid, violent confrontational race that has happened over the last 2,000 years and to go in a new direction where we see the world as one and that other people's good fortune is my good fortune, not a loss to me, then I expect that someone holding a conversation in this room in 30-40 years will be even happier than you and I are.

About Alan Macfarlane

Alan Macfarlane was born in Assam, India, in 1941, the son of a manager of a tea plantation. He went to the Dragon School in Oxford and Sedbergh School in Yorkshire. He got a B.A. in history at Oxford in 1963. He gained doctorates in history (Oxford, 1967) and anthropology (London, 1972) and has taught at the University of Cambridge since 1971 where he was at first for four years a Senior Research Fellow at King's College. He became a Reader in Historical Anthropology in 1981, a Fellow of the British Academy in 1986 and a Professor of Anthropological Science at Cambridge University in 1991. He is currently Emeritus Professor of Anthropological Science and Life Fellow of King's College, Cambridge.

He has given the Frazer, Malinowski, Marett and Huxley Lectures in Britain, the Silver Jubilee Guest Lecture at the Delhi School of Economics, the Sir Li Ka-shing Distinguished Lectures in China and the Maruyama Lectures at Berkeley. He gave the Wang Guowei Lectures in China in 2012 and the Luoja Lecture at Wuhan University in 2014. He has taught at the University of Tokyo and lectured at a number of Japanese, Chinese and American universities.

Alan has undertaken extensive historical and anthropological work in England, Nagaland, Nepal, Japan and China, which has led to a number of multimedia projects and the development of computer databases. Some of his books are listed below. His website (www.alanmacfarlane.com) contains interviews of over 260 leading academics and thinkers, as well as many academic seminars and lectures, training films, films from around the world, and various historical and anthropological databases and sets of writings. Many of his films are up on YouTube. His work is done in collaboration with his wife and colleague, Sarah Harrison. He is currently one of the directors of the Cambridge Rivers Project at King's College Cambridge, working extensively with Chinese colleagues, in particular Wang Zilan, having travelled to China seventeen times since 1996.

Selected books by Alan Macfarlane

Witchcraft in Tudor and Stuart England (1970)

The Family Life of Ralph Josselin (1970)

(ed.), *The Diary of Ralph Josselin* (1976)

Resources and Population: A Study of the Gurungs of Central Nepal (1976)

Reconstructing Historical Communities (1977)

An Introduction to English Historical Records (1983)

The Origins of English Individualism (1978)

The Justice and the Mare's Ale: Law and Disorder in Seventeenth Century England (1981)

Marriage and Love in England (1986)

The Culture of Capitalism (1987)

The Savage Wars of Peace: England, Japan and the Malthusian Trap (1997)

The Riddle of the Modern World: Of Liberty, Wealth and Equality (2000)

The Making of the Modern World (2002)

(with Gerry Martin), *The Glass Bathyscaphe: How Glass Changed the World* (2002)

(with Iris Macfarlane), *Green Gold: The Empire of Tea* (2003)

Letters to Lily: On How the World Works (2005)

Japan Through the Looking Glass (2007)

Reflections on Cambridge (2009)

The Invention of the Modern World (2013)

China, Japan, Europe and the Anglo-sphere: A Comparative Analysis (2018)

Understanding the Chinese: A Personal A-Z (2020)

(with Richard Marshall) *Understandings of the Modern World* (2023)

About Tim Yip

Through his prolific works in art, film, theatre and literature, Tim Yip has honed his thesis New Orientalism, which proposes that – far from being determined – supposed boundaries of geography and time are porous. For "Crouching Tiger, Hidden Dragon" (dir. Ang Lee, 1999), Tim won the Oscar for "Best Art Direction", and the BAFTA award for "Best Costume Design". Tim has worked with some of the greatest auteurs in East Asian cinema, including John Woo and Tsai Ming-liang. In the field of theatre, Tim has collaborated with Robert Wilson, Akram Khan, Zhang Yimou, Stan Lai, and Yang Liping to name a few. His directed plays "Storm in Emptiness" and "Love in a Fallen City" are a merge of video and stage art named Total Art Theatre.

Tim has had exhibitions worldwide including the National Palace Museum Taipei, Maison de la Culture de Bourges (France), the Royal Dutch Theater (Holland), the Madrid Cultural Center (Spain), and the Kennedy Center for the Performing Arts (US), New York International Asian Art Fair, Beijing Today Art Museum, MOMA (Taiwan), Esplanade (Singapore), Maison de la Culture D'Amiens (France), Shanghai Power Station of Art and Southbank Centre London.

Tim was invited to be the designer of Team China's Olympic Podium Uniform in 2020 Tokyo Olympics and 2022 Beijing Winter Olympics. He was also the set and costume designer of Opera "Lohengrin" directed by François Girard. The opera had its premiere at the Bolshoi Theatre of Russia in 2022 and The Metropolitan Opera House US in 2023. Recently he has designed an exhibition in the Minneapolis Institute of Art "Eternal Offerings: Chinese Ritual Bronzes".

In addition to visual art, Tim has also devoted to writing for many years, with publication include "Lost in Time", "Flowers of the Wind", "Floating", "Connections", "Rouge: L'Art de Tim Yip", "GIJON", "Illusions of Silence", "Passage", "Reformation: The

Aesthetics of Tim Yip", "Mirror" and more. His books have been translated into English, French and other languages, and were published worldwide. Yip's latest publication is "Mirror" (simplified Chinese version).

Selected works by Tim Yip

Production and Costume Designer, Temptation of a Monk, directed by Clara Law (1993)

Costume Designer, Rashomon, Buhnen Graz Opera House, Austria, directed by Lin Hwai-Min (1996)

Production and Costume Designer, Crouching Tiger Hidden Dragon, directed by Ang Lee (2000)

Costume Designer, Athens Olympics Beijing Handover Performance, directed by Zhang Yimou (2004)

Set & Costume Designer, Palace of Eternal Youth, Suzhou Kunqu Opera Theatre of Jiangsu Province (2004)

Production and Costume Designer, The Banquet, directed by Feng Xiaogang (2006)

Production and Costume Designer, Red Cliff I & II, directed by John Woo (2008)

Costume Designer, 1433 - The Grand Voyage, directed by Robert Wilson with U Theatre (2010)

Set & Costume Designer, Jiaofang Ji by Han Tang Yue Fu Music and Dance Ensemble (2011)

Costume Designer, A Dream Like A Dream, directed by Stan Lai (2013)

Costume Designer, The Han Show, directed by Franco Dragone (2014)

Costume Designer, Marco Polo, Season One and Two, Netflix Series, created by John Fusco (2014/2016)

Art Director & Costume Designer, Under Siege, Yang Liping Company, directed by Yang Liping (2015)

Set & Costume Designer, Dream of the Red Chamber, San Francisco Opera, composed by Bright Sheng, directed by Stan Lai (2016)

Set & Costume Designer, Giselle, English National Ballet, choreographed by Akram Khan (2016)

Concept, Director and Visual Designer, Storm in Emptiness, Multimedia Theatre (2017)

Set & Costume Designer, The Great Gatsby, Hong Kong Ballet, choreographed by Septime Webre (2019)

Original Production Concept Designer, Dragon Spring Phoenix Rise, The Shed in New York, directed by Chen Shi-Zheng (2019)

Designer of Team China's Olympic Podium Uniform, 2020 Tokyo Olympics and 2022 Beijing Winter Olympics (2020/2022)

Chief Director & Visual Designer, Love in a Fallen City (2021)

Set & Costume Designer, Lohengrin, The Historic Stage of the Bolshoi Theatre of Russia in Moscow and The Metropolitan Opera House in New York, directed by Francois Girard (2022/2023)

Exhibition Designer, Eternal Offerings: Chinese Ritual Bronzes, Minneapolis Institute of Art (2023)

Production and Costume Designer, Fengshen Trilogy aka Creation of the Gods, directed by Wu Ershan (2023)

Acknowledgements

We would like to thank the following for their great efforts in making this book possible.

Special thanks to Yuchen Qin , Dalong Ge, and MUYE design team for crafting its visual appeal. The invaluable support from Tim Yip's assistants, Yuanshan Guo and Yuan Gao, ensured smooth coordination throughout.

We'd like to express our appreciation to Yue Li and the China Cam Rivers Team for their dedication, as well as Zilan Wang and Levente Koroes at the Cam Rivers Office in the U.K. for their unwavering commitment.

Irene Galstian's finesse with the text has been instrumental, and Sarah Harrison's guidance has been indispensable. A nod to Lili, for her calming inspiration.

Lastly, heartfelt thanks to Tim Yip for granting us the privilege of using his artworks in this book.

Printed in Great Britain
by Amazon

38613759R00126